Python API Development with Flask

Build APIs They'll Love: The Flask Advantage! Master Flask Endpoints, Data Handling, and Deployment!

Katie Millie

Python API Development with Flask

Build APIs They'll Love: The Flask Advantage! Master Flask Endpoints, Data Handling, and Deployment!

By

Katie Millie

Copyright notice

Copyright © 2024 Katie Millie. All rights reserved.

Every aspect of this publication is protected by copyright law and may not be replicated, disseminated, or conveyed through any medium, whether it be photocopying, recording, or other electronic or mechanical methods, without explicit written consent from the author. The sole exceptions to this rule are brief quotations incorporated within critical reviews and specific noncommercial uses allowed by copyright law. For inquiries regarding permissions, please reach out to Katie Millie directly. Any unauthorized utilization or reproduction of this material is strictly forbidden and may lead to legal consequences. Your adherence to these guidelines is greatly appreciated and essential for upholding the author's intellectual property rights.

Table of Contents

INTRODUCTION

Chapter 1

    Why Flask for APIs? The Allure of Flexibility

        Core Concepts: Routes, Views, and Templates Explained in Flask

            Setting Up Your Development Environment for Flask API Development

                Hello, World! Building Your First Flask API

Chapter 2

    Application Structure: Laying the Foundation for Growth

        Blueprints: Modularizing Your API for Maintainability

            Dependency Injection: Keeping Your Code Clean and Organized

                Configuration Management: Secrets Deserve a Safe Place

Chapter 3

    RESTful Design Principles: Building a Consistent and Predictable API

        HTTP Methods in Action: Verbs that Power Your API (GET, POST, PUT, DELETE)

            Resource-Oriented Design: Structuring Endpoints Around Your Data

                Versioning Your API: Ensuring Smooth Transitions and Backward Compatibility

Chapter 4

    Working with Data: From Simple Variables to Databases with SQLAlchemy

Data Validation: Ensuring Your API Receives Clean Information
- Serialization: Transforming Data for Seamless Consumption by Clients
  - Common Data Formats: JSON, XML, and Beyond

Chapter 5
Understanding Authentication Mechanisms: Basic, Token-Based, and More
- Implementing Authentication with Flask Extensions
  - Session Management: Keeping Users Logged In

Chapter 6
Role-Based Access Control (RBAC): Granular Control Over User Permissions
- Protecting Specific Resources and Endpoints
  - Best Practices for Secure Authorization

Chapter 7
Unit Testing: Isolating and Validating Individual Components
- Integration Testing: Ensuring Different Parts of Your API Work Together Seamlessly
  - Test-Driven Development (TDD): A Proactive Approach to Building Robust APIs
    - Popular Testing Frameworks for Flask: Unittest, pytest, and More

Chapter 8
Setting Up a Local Development Server for Testing and Iteration
- Deployment Options: Cloud Platforms like

- Heroku and AWS
  - Configuration Management for Production Environments
    - Monitoring and Logging: Keeping an Eye on Your Deployed API

Chapter 9
- Clean Coding Principles: Writing Code You (and Others) Can Love
  - Code Formatting and Linting: Enforcing Consistency and Style
    - Documentation: The User Manual for Your API

Chapter 10
- Flask Extensions: Supercharge Your Development with Powerful Tools
  - Marshmallow: Effortless Data Serialization and Validation
    - Other Useful Extensions for Common Tasks

Conclusion
- Appendix
  - Glossary of terms
    - Common Flask API Development Pitfalls (and How to Avoid Them!)

INTRODUCTION

Python's Powerhouse: Building APIs with Flask

Ever dreamt of creating the invisible backbone of the next big app? The one that seamlessly connects users, data, and functionality through the magic of APIs? Well, fellow Pythonista, prepare to unleash your inner API architect! This book is your gateway to mastering Flask, the Python microframework that's become a developer's dream tool for crafting clean, powerful, and secure APIs.

Forget about clunky, overbearing frameworks. Flask empowers you to be the artist, not a slave to a rigid system. It grants you the freedom to design, build, and scale your API with elegance and efficiency. But fear not, whether you're a seasoned Pythonista or just starting your coding journey, this book caters to all!

Perhaps these questions are swirling in your mind:

- How do I structure my API for clarity and future growth?
- What are the secret ingredients for crafting powerful endpoints?
- Security: How do I keep my API safe from prying eyes?
- And the ultimate question: How do I write clean, maintainable code that future me (or anyone on my team) can understand?

This book is your roadmap to conquering these challenges and more. We'll be your guide as you:

- **Forge a Flawless Foundation:** Learn the core principles of Flask API development, from structuring your application to wielding the power of Blueprints for modularity.
- **Sculpt Meaningful Endpoints:** Master the art of designing intuitive and RESTful endpoints that make perfect sense to you and anyone using your API.
- **Embrace the Power of Data:** Explore effective data handling techniques, from working with databases like SQLAlchemy to crafting elegant data validation and serialization.
- **Security: Your API's Shield:** Delve into the essential security measures to protect your API from unauthorized access and vulnerabilities. Learn about authentication, authorization, and best practices to keep your data safe.
- **Testing: Building Confidence:** Discover the importance of unit and integration testing, and equip yourself with the tools to write robust tests that ensure your API functions flawlessly.
- **Deployment: Sharing Your Creation:** Learn the secrets of deploying your API to the real world, whether on a local server or a cloud platform.

But this book isn't just about technical prowess. We'll also explore the art of clean coding, design patterns that promote maintainability, and the importance of clear documentation – because even the most brilliant code needs a user manual!

We'll unveil the power of tools like Flask-RESTful and Marshmallow to streamline your development process. We'll even sprinkle in some real-world examples to show you how these concepts come to life.

So, are you ready to unleash the full potential of Flask for API development? Are you eager to craft APIs that are not just functional, but elegant, secure, and a joy to work with? Then turn the page and let's embark on this exciting journey together!

Chapter 1

Why Flask for APIs? The Allure of Flexibility

Flask, a lightweight web framework for Python, has gained immense popularity for API development. Its simplicity, flexibility, and powerful extension ecosystem make it an ideal choice for developers looking to build robust APIs. In this essay, we will explore the reasons behind Flask's popularity for API development, its key features, and some example code to illustrate its capabilities.

Simplicity and Minimalism

Flask is known for its simplicity and minimalist design. Unlike some other frameworks that come with a lot of built-in features, Flask provides the essentials and leaves the rest to the developer. This minimalism is a significant advantage when developing APIs because it allows developers to start small and scale their applications as needed.

Example: Basic Flask API

Here is a simple example of a Flask API:

```python
```

```
from flask import Flask, jsonify, request

app = Flask(__name__)

@app.route('/api/greet', methods=['GET'])
def greet():
    name = request.args.get('name', 'World')
    return jsonify(message=f'Hello, {name}!')

if __name__ == '__main__':
    app.run(debug=True)
```

In this example, we create a basic API endpoint `/api/greet` that accepts a `GET` request with a query parameter `name`. If the `name` parameter is not provided, it defaults to 'World'. The API responds with a JSON message. This simplicity in setting up an API is one of Flask's key attractions.

Flexibility and Extensibility

Flask's design philosophy emphasizes flexibility. It does not impose a specific way of organizing your code or restrict you to a particular pattern. This flexibility allows developers to structure their applications in a way that best suits their needs.

Moreover, Flask's extensibility is facilitated through a rich ecosystem of extensions. Whether you need to add authentication, database integration, or API documentation, Flask has an extension for it. Some popular extensions include Flask-SQLAlchemy for database management, Flask-JWT for JSON Web Token authentication, and Flask-RESTful for building REST APIs.

Example: Extending Flask with Flask-RESTful

Flask-RESTful is an extension that adds support for quickly building REST APIs. Here's how you can use it to enhance the previous example:

```python
from flask import Flask, request
from flask_restful import Resource, Api

app = Flask(__name__)
api = Api(app)

class Greet(Resource):
    def get(self):
        name = request.args.get('name', 'World')
        return {'message': f'Hello, {name}!'}

api.add_resource(Greet, '/api/greet')
```

```
if __name__ == '__main__':
    app.run(debug=True)
```

With Flask-RESTful, the API structure becomes more modular. The `Greet` class encapsulates the logic for the `/api/greet` endpoint, making the code cleaner and easier to maintain.

Lightweight and Fast

Flask is lightweight and fast, which makes it suitable for building APIs that require high performance and low latency. It does not include unnecessary overhead, allowing you to create efficient applications. This performance advantage is particularly important for APIs, where response time and resource utilization are critical factors.

Example: Middleware for Performance Monitoring

You can easily add middleware to monitor the performance of your Flask API. Here's an example of how to log request processing time:

```python
from flask import Flask, request, g
```

```python
import time

app = Flask(__name__)

@app.before_request
def start_timer():
    g.start = time.time()

@app.after_request
def log_request(response):
    elapsed_time = time.time() - g.start
    app.logger.info(f'Request to {request.path} took {elapsed_time} seconds')
    return response

@app.route('/api/greet', methods=['GET'])
def greet():
    name = request.args.get('name', 'World')
    return jsonify(message=f'Hello, {name}!')

if __name__ == '__main__':
    app.run(debug=True)
```
```

In this example, we use the `before_request` and `after_request` hooks to measure and log the time taken to process each request. This kind of middleware can
```

help you keep track of performance and identify bottlenecks.

Community and Documentation

Flask has a large and active community, which means you can find plenty of resources, tutorials, and third-party tools to help you with your API development. The official Flask documentation is comprehensive and well-organized, making it easy for developers of all skill levels to get started and find the information they need.

Flask's allure for API development lies in its simplicity, flexibility, and powerful extension ecosystem. Its minimalist design allows developers to start small and scale their applications as needed, while its extensibility ensures that additional functionality can be easily integrated. The lightweight nature of Flask makes it suitable for high-performance applications, and its active community provides ample support and resources.

Whether you are building a simple API or a complex web service, Flask provides the tools and flexibility you need to succeed. Its combination of ease of use, scalability, and performance makes it an excellent choice for Python developers looking to create robust and efficient APIs.

Core Concepts: Routes, Views, and Templates Explained in Flask

Flask is a micro web framework for Python that is simple yet powerful, making it a popular choice for web development. To effectively use Flask, it's crucial to understand its core concepts: routes, views, and templates. These components form the backbone of any Flask application. In this essay, we will delve into these concepts and illustrate their use with code examples focused on API development.

Routes

In Flask, routes are used to map URLs to functions in your Python code. This mapping is essential for defining how different URLs should be handled by your application.

Example: Basic Route

Here's a simple example of a Flask route:

```python
from flask import Flask

app = Flask(__name__)
```

```
@app.route('/')
def home():
    return "Welcome to the Home Page"

if __name__ == '__main__':
    app.run(debug=True)
```

In this example, the `@app.route('/')` decorator defines a route for the root URL (`/`). When this URL is accessed, the `home` function is called, returning the text "Welcome to the Home Page". This basic setup is the foundation for handling different URLs in a Flask application.

Example: Route with Parameter

Routes can also include parameters, which allow you to capture values from the URL:

```python
@app.route('/user/<username>')
def show_user_profile(username):
    return f"User: {username}"
```

Here, `<username>` is a dynamic part of the URL. When a user accesses `/user/john`, the `show_user_profile` function is called with `username` set to `john`.

Views

In Flask, views are the functions associated with routes. These functions are responsible for handling the logic and returning the response for a specific URL.

Example: View Function

Let's enhance the previous example with a view function that returns JSON data:

```python
from flask import jsonify

@app.route('/api/user/<username>')
def get_user(username):
    user_data = {
        'username': username,
        'email': f'{username}@example.com'
    }
    return jsonify(user_data)
```

In this example, the `get_user` function is a view that returns JSON data for a given username. The `jsonify` function converts the dictionary to a JSON response, which is a common format for APIs.

Templates

Templates in Flask are used to render HTML. They allow you to separate the presentation logic from the business logic, promoting a clean and maintainable codebase. Flask uses Jinja2 as its template engine.

Example: Basic Template

First, let's create a basic HTML template. Save this as `templates/user.html`:

```html
<!doctype html>
<html lang="en">
  <head>
    <title>User Profile</title>
  </head>
  <body>
    <h1>User: {{ username }}</h1>
    <p>Email: {{ email }}</p>
  </body>
</html>
```

```

Now, let's modify our Flask app to use this template:

```python
from flask import render_template

@app.route('/user/<username>')
def show_user_profile(username):
    user_data = {
        'username': username,
        'email': f'{username}@example.com'
    }
    return render_template('user.html', **user_data)
```

In this example, the `show_user_profile` function renders the `user.html` template, passing `username` and `email` as variables. The `render_template` function integrates the data with the template and returns the resulting HTML.

Example: Combining Routes, Views, and Templates

Let's create a more comprehensive example that combines all three concepts:

```python

```python
from flask import Flask, render_template, jsonify, request

app = Flask(__name__)

# Route for the home page
@app.route('/')
def home():
    return "Welcome to the API Home Page"

# API route returning JSON data
@app.route('/api/user/<username>', methods=['GET'])
def get_user(username):
    user_data = {
        'username': username,
        'email': f'{username}@example.com'
    }
    return jsonify(user_data)

# Route rendering an HTML template
@app.route('/user/<username>')
def show_user_profile(username):
    user_data = {
        'username': username,
        'email': f'{username}@example.com'
    }
    return render_template('user.html', **user_data)
```

```
if __name__ == '__main__':
    app.run(debug=True)
```
```

In this combined example:

- The root route ('/') returns a simple welcome message.

- The `/api/user/<username>` route returns JSON data for the specified user.

- The `/user/<username>` route renders an HTML page using a template.

## Advanced Topics: Adding Forms and Handling Requests

To extend the functionality, you might want to include forms and handle POST requests in your views.

### Example: Handling POST Requests

Let's add a form to our template and handle its submission in a new route.

First, update `templates/user.html` to include a form:
```

```html
<!doctype html>
<html lang="en">
  <head>
    <title>User Profile</title>
  </head>
  <body>
    <h1>User: {{ username }}</h1>
    <p>Email: {{ email }}</p>
    <form action="/user" method="post">
      <input type="text" name="username" placeholder="Enter username">
      <button type="submit">Submit</button>
    </form>
  </body>
</html>
```

Next, create a route to handle the form submission:

```python
@app.route('/user', methods=['POST'])
def update_user():
    username = request.form['username']
    user_data = {
        'username': username,
        'email': f'{username}@example.com'
    }
```

```
    return render_template('user.html', **user_data)
```

In this example:

- The form in `user.html` submits a POST request to `/user`.

- The `update_user` view handles the form submission, retrieves the `username` from the form data, and renders the `user.html` template with the updated user data.

Understanding the core concepts of routes, views, and templates is essential for developing applications with Flask. Routes map URLs to view functions, views handle the logic and return responses, and templates render HTML. Together, these components provide a powerful and flexible framework for building both simple and complex web applications. By mastering these concepts, you can harness the full potential of Flask to create robust, maintainable, and scalable applications.

Setting Up Your Development Environment for Flask API Development

Setting up a robust development environment is crucial for building reliable and maintainable applications. Flask, being a micro web framework for Python, requires a well-configured setup to ensure smooth development and testing. This essay will guide you through setting up your development environment for Flask API development, covering everything from installing Python to setting up a virtual environment, installing Flask, creating a basic project structure, and using version control.

Prerequisites

Before you start, ensure you have Python installed on your machine. Flask is compatible with Python 3.6 and above. You can download Python from the official website [python.org](https://www.python.org/).

Checking Python Installation

To check if Python is installed, open your terminal or command prompt and run:

```bash
python --version
```

If Python is installed, you should see the version number. If not, download and install it from the official website.

Setting Up a Virtual Environment

A virtual environment allows you to create an isolated space for your project dependencies, ensuring that your project has all the necessary packages without interfering with other projects or system-wide packages.

Creating a Virtual Environment

To create a virtual environment, navigate to your project directory and run:

```bash
python -m venv venv
```

Here, `venv` is the name of the virtual environment folder. You can choose any name you prefer.

Activating the Virtual Environment

Activate the virtual environment using the following command:

- On Windows:

  ```bash
  venv\Scripts\activate
  ```

- On macOS/Linux:

  ```bash
  source venv/bin/activate
  ```

Once activated, your terminal prompt will change to indicate that you are now working within the virtual environment.

Installing Flask

With the virtual environment activated, install Flask using `pip`:

```bash
pip install flask
```

This command installs Flask and its dependencies.

Creating a Basic Project Structure

A well-organized project structure is essential for maintaining and scaling your application. Here's a recommended structure for a Flask API project:

```
my_flask_api/
│
├── venv/
├── app/
│   ├── __init__.py
│   ├── routes.py
│   ├── models.py
│   ├── config.py
│   └── templates/
│       └── index.html
├── tests/
│   └── test_routes.py
├── .gitignore
├── requirements.txt
└── run.py
```

Creating the Project Files

1. `run.py`: The entry point for your Flask application.

   ```python
   ```

```
from app import create_app

app = create_app()

if __name__ == '__main__':
    app.run(debug=True)
```

2. `app/__init__.py`: Initializes the Flask application and sets up configurations.

```python
from flask import Flask

def create_app():
    app = Flask(__name__)
    app.config.from_pyfile('config.py')

    from .routes import main
    app.register_blueprint(main)

    return app
```

3. `app/config.py`: Contains configuration settings for your Flask application.

```python
```

```python
import os

class Config:
    SECRET_KEY = os.urandom(24)
    DEBUG = True
```

4. **`app/routes.py`**: Defines the routes for your API.

```python
from flask import Blueprint, jsonify

main = Blueprint('main', __name__)

@main.route('/')
def index():
    return jsonify(message="Welcome to the Flask API")
```

5. **`requirements.txt`**: Lists the project dependencies.

```
flask
```

6. **`.gitignore`**: Specifies files and directories to be ignored by Git.

```
venv/
__pycache__/
*.pyc
```

7. **`tests/test_routes.py`**: Contains tests for your routes.

```python
import unittest
from app import create_app

class RoutesTestCase(unittest.TestCase):

    def setUp(self):
        self.app = create_app()
        self.client = self.app.test_client()

    def test_index(self):
        response = self.client.get('/')
        self.assertEqual(response.status_code, 200)
        self.assertIn('Welcome to the Flask API', response.get_data(as_text=True))

    if __name__ == '__main__':
        unittest.main()
```

Using Version Control

Version control is essential for tracking changes and collaborating with other developers. Git is a widely-used version control system. Initialize a Git repository in your project directory:

```bash
git init
```

Add your files to the repository and make the initial commit:

```bash
git add .
git commit -m "Initial commit"
```

Running Your Application

With everything set up, you can now run your Flask application. Ensure your virtual environment is activated, then execute:

```bash
python run.py
```

```

Open your browser and navigate to `http://127.0.0.1:5000/` to see your Flask API in action.

Setting up a development environment for Flask API development involves several key steps, including installing Python, creating and activating a virtual environment, installing Flask, organizing your project structure, and using version control. By following these steps, you create a solid foundation for your Flask application, making it easier to manage dependencies, maintain code quality, and collaborate with others. This setup not only enhances productivity but also ensures that your development process is smooth and efficient, allowing you to focus on building robust and scalable APIs.

## Hello, World! Building Your First Flask API

Flask, a lightweight and powerful web framework for Python, is an excellent choice for building APIs. Its simplicity and flexibility allow developers to start small and scale as needed. This tutorial will guide you through creating your first Flask API, starting with a "Hello, World!" endpoint and extending to a more complex API with multiple routes and data handling.

### Setting Up Your Environment
```

Before diving into the code, ensure you have Python installed. Flask works with Python 3.6 and above. You can download Python from the official [python.org](https://www.python.org/) website.

Installing Flask

First, create a project directory and navigate to it:

```bash
mkdir my_flask_api
cd my_flask_api
```

Next, set up a virtual environment to manage your project's dependencies:

```bash
python -m venv venv
```

Activate the virtual environment:

- On Windows:

  ```bash
  venv\Scripts\activate
  ```

```

- On macOS/Linux:

  ```bash
  source venv/bin/activate
  ```

With the virtual environment activated, install Flask:

```bash
pip install flask
```

Creating Your First Flask API

Now that your environment is set up, let's create a basic Flask API. We'll start with the quintessential "Hello, World!" example.

Project Structure

Organize your project as follows:

```
my_flask_api/
│
├── venv/
```
```

```
├── app/
│   ├── __init__.py
│   └── routes.py
├── .gitignore
├── requirements.txt
└── run.py
```

Creating the Application

1. `run.py`: This is the entry point of your application.

   ```python
   from app import create_app

   app = create_app()

   if __name__ == '__main__':
       app.run(debug=True)
   ```

2. `app/__init__.py`: This file initializes the Flask application and sets up configurations and routes.

   ```python
   from flask import Flask

   def create_app():
   ```

```
    app = Flask(__name__)

    from .routes import main
    app.register_blueprint(main)

    return app
```

3. **`app/routes.py`**: Define the routes for your API here.

```python
from flask import Blueprint, jsonify

main = Blueprint('main', __name__)

@main.route('/')
def hello_world():
    return jsonify(message="Hello, World!")
```

4. **`.gitignore`**: List files and directories to be ignored by Git.

```
venv/
__pycache__/
*.pyc
```

5. `requirements.txt`: List your project dependencies.

```
Flask
```

Running the Application

With the structure and code in place, run your Flask application:

```bash
python run.py
```

Open your browser and navigate to `http://127.0.0.1:5000/`. You should see a JSON response:

```json
{
   "message": "Hello, World!"
}
```

Extending the API

Now that we have a basic Flask API running, let's extend it by adding more routes and handling data.

Adding More Routes

We'll add a route to handle user data. Update `app/routes.py` to include new endpoints.

1. Updating `app/routes.py`:

```python
from flask import Blueprint, jsonify, request

main = Blueprint('main', __name__)

@main.route('/')
def hello_world():
    return jsonify(message="Hello, World!")

@main.route('/api/user/<username>', methods=['GET'])
def get_user(username):
    user_data = {
        'username': username,
        'email': f'{username}@example.com'
    }
    return jsonify(user_data)
```

```
@main.route('/api/user', methods=['POST'])
def create_user():
    data = request.get_json()
    username = data.get('username')
    email = data.get('email')
    return jsonify(message=f'User {username} with email {email} created successfully'), 201
```

2. Testing New Routes:

- To get user data, navigate to `http://127.0.0.1:5000/api/user/<username>`, replacing `<username>` with a desired username. You should see a JSON response with user data.

- To create a new user, you can use a tool like `curl` or Postman to send a POST request:

```bash
curl -X POST http://127.0.0.1:5000/api/user -H "Content-Type: application/json" -d '{"username": "john", "email": "john@example.com"}'
```

This should return a JSON response indicating that the user was created successfully.

Handling Errors

To make the API more robust, we should handle potential errors gracefully.

1. Updating `app/routes.py` to Handle Errors:

```python
from flask import Blueprint, jsonify, request, abort

main = Blueprint('main', __name__)

@main.route('/')
def hello_world():
    return jsonify(message="Hello, World!")

@main.route('/api/user/<username>', methods=['GET'])
def get_user(username):
    user_data = {
        'username': username,
        'email': f'{username}@example.com'
    }
    return jsonify(user_data)

@main.route('/api/user', methods=['POST'])
def create_user():
    if not request.is_json:
```

```
        abort(400, description="Invalid request format.
JSON required.")

    data = request.get_json()
    if 'username' not in data or 'email' not in data:
        abort(400, description="Missing required fields:
'username' and 'email'.")

    username = data['username']
    email = data['email']
    return jsonify(message=f'User {username} with
email {email} created successfully'), 201

@main.errorhandler(400)
def bad_request(error):
    return jsonify(error=str(error)), 400
```

2. Testing Error Handling: Send a POST request without JSON data to test the error handling:

```bash
curl -X POST http://127.0.0.1:5000/api/user -H "Content-Type: application/json"
```

This should return a JSON error message indicating an invalid request format.

- Send a POST request with missing fields to test the field validation:

```bash
curl -X POST http://127.0.0.1:5000/api/user -H "Content-Type: application/json" -d '{"username": "john"}'
```

This should return a JSON error message indicating the missing required fields.

Adding Unit Tests

Testing is an essential part of development to ensure that your API behaves as expected. We'll add some basic tests using the `unittest` framework.

1. Creating a Test Directory and Files:

Create a `tests` directory with a file named `test_routes.py`:

```
my_flask_api/
├── tests/
│   └── test_routes.py
```

```

## 2. Writing Tests in `tests/test_routes.py`:

```python
import unittest
from app import create_app

class RoutesTestCase(unittest.TestCase):

    def setUp(self):
        self.app = create_app()
        self.client = self.app.test_client()
        self.app.testing = True

    def test_hello_world(self):
        response = self.client.get('/')
        self.assertEqual(response.status_code, 200)
        self.assertIn('Hello, World!', response.get_data(as_text=True))

    def test_get_user(self):
        response = self.client.get('/api/user/john')
        self.assertEqual(response.status_code, 200)
        data = response.get_json()
        self.assertEqual(data['username'], 'john')
        self.assertEqual(data['email'], 'john@example.com')

```
    def test_create_user(self):
        response = self.client.post('/api/user', json={'username': 'john', 'email': 'john@example.com'})
        self.assertEqual(response.status_code, 201)
        self.assertIn('User john with email john@example.com created successfully', response.get_data(as_text=True))

if __name__ == '__main__':
    unittest.main()
```

3. Running the Tests:

Run the tests with:

```bash
python -m unittest discover tests
```

This command will discover and run all the tests in the `tests` directory, providing feedback on the success or failure of each test.

Building your first Flask API involves setting up a development environment, creating a basic project structure, defining routes and views, handling errors, and writing tests. Flask's simplicity and flexibility make it an excellent choice for developing APIs. By following this tutorial, you've created a basic but functional Flask API that can be easily extended and customized to fit more complex requirements. This foundation provides a solid starting point for any web or API development project using Flask.

Chapter 2

Application Structure: Laying the Foundation for Growth

When developing a Flask API, a well-organized application structure is crucial for scalability, maintainability, and ease of collaboration. A robust structure not only helps manage growing codebases but also facilitates testing, deployment, and future enhancements. This guide will walk you through setting up a structured Flask application, detailing each component with code examples.

Why Structure Matters

A clear and logical project structure ensures:

- **Maintainability**: Easy to navigate and update the codebase.

- **Scalability**: Supports adding new features and modules without significant refactoring.

- **Collaboration**: Facilitates teamwork by providing a common framework and conventions.

- Testing: Simplifies writing and running tests for various components.

Recommended Project Structure

Here's a comprehensive structure for a scalable Flask application:

```
my_flask_api/
│
├── venv/
├── app/
│   ├── __init__.py
│   ├── config.py
│   ├── models.py
│   ├── routes/
│   │   ├── __init__.py
│   │   ├── user_routes.py
│   ├── templates/
│   │   └── index.html
├── tests/
│   ├── __init__.py
│   ├── test_user_routes.py
├── migrations/
│   └── README.md
├── .gitignore
├── requirements.txt
```

```
├── run.py
└── README.md
```

Directory Breakdown

- `venv/`: Virtual environment directory, isolated Python environment for dependencies.

- `app/`: Main application folder containing all code related to the Flask app.

- `__init__.py`: Initializes the Flask app and includes setup configurations.

- `config.py`: Configuration settings for different environments.

- `models.py`: Database models.

- `routes/`: Contains route handlers grouped by functionality.

- `__init__.py`: Initializes the routes module.

- `user_routes.py`: Example route file for user-related endpoints.

- `templates/`: HTML templates for rendering views.

- `tests/`: Contains unit and integration tests.

- `__init__.py`: Initializes the tests module.

- `test_user_routes.py`: Example test file for user routes.

- `migrations/`: Directory for database migrations.

- `.gitignore`: Specifies files and directories to be ignored by Git.

- `requirements.txt`: Lists project dependencies.

- `run.py`: Entry point for running the Flask application.

- `README.md`: Project documentation.

Setting Up the Application

1. Initializing the Flask App

Create `app/__init__.py` to initialize the Flask app and set up configurations:

```python
from flask import Flask
from flask_sqlalchemy import SQLAlchemy
from flask_migrate import Migrate

db = SQLAlchemy()
migrate = Migrate()

def create_app():
    app = Flask(__name__)
    app.config.from_object('app.config.Config')

    db.init_app(app)
    migrate.init_app(app, db)

    from app.routes import user_routes
    app.register_blueprint(user_routes.bp)

    return app
```

2. Configuration Settings

Create `app/config.py` to manage different configuration settings:

```python
```

```
import os

class Config:
    SECRET_KEY = os.environ.get('SECRET_KEY', 'default_secret_key')
    SQLALCHEMY_DATABASE_URI = os.environ.get('DATABASE_URL', 'sqlite:///app.db')
    SQLALCHEMY_TRACK_MODIFICATIONS = False
```

3. Database Models

Create `app/models.py` to define your database models:

```python
from app import db

class User(db.Model):
    id = db.Column(db.Integer, primary_key=True)
    username = db.Column(db.String(64), unique=True, nullable=False)
    email = db.Column(db.String(120), unique=True, nullable=False)

    def __repr__(self):
        return f'<User {self.username}>'
```

4. Routes and Blueprints

Create `app/routes/__init__.py` to initialize the routes module:

```python
# app/routes/__init__.py
# This file can be empty, or you can add initialization code if needed.
```

Create `app/routes/user_routes.py` for user-related routes:

```python
from flask import Blueprint, jsonify, request
from app import db
from app.models import User

bp = Blueprint('user', __name__)

@bp.route('/api/users', methods=['GET'])
def get_users():
    users = User.query.all()
    return jsonify([{'id': user.id, 'username': user.username, 'email': user.email} for user in users])
```

```python
@bp.route('/api/users', methods=['POST'])
def create_user():
    data = request.get_json()
    new_user = User(username=data['username'], email=data['email'])
    db.session.add(new_user)
    db.session.commit()
    return jsonify({'id': new_user.id, 'username': new_user.username, 'email': new_user.email}), 201
```

5. Entry Point

Create `run.py` as the entry point for your application:

```python
from app import create_app

app = create_app()

if __name__ == '__main__':
    app.run(debug=True)
```

6. Requirements and Gitignore

Create `requirements.txt` to list project dependencies:

```
Flask
Flask-SQLAlchemy
Flask-Migrate
```

Create `.gitignore` to specify files and directories to ignore:

```
venv/
__pycache__/
*.pyc
instance/
.mypy_cache/
.pytest_cache/
*.db
```

7. Testing

Create `tests/__init__.py` to initialize the tests module:

```python
# tests/__init__.py
# This file can be empty, or you can add initialization
code if needed.
```

Create `tests/test_user_routes.py` to test user routes:

```python
import unittest
from app import create_app, db
from app.models import User

class UserRoutesTestCase(unittest.TestCase):

    def setUp(self):
        self.app = create_app()
        self.app.config['TESTING'] = True

self.app.config['SQLALCHEMY_DATABASE_URI'] = 'sqlite:///:memory:'
        self.client = self.app.test_client()

        with self.app.app_context():
            db.create_all()

    def tearDown(self):
        with self.app.app_context():
            db.session.remove()
            db.drop_all()

    def test_get_users(self):
        response = self.client.get('/api/users')
```

```
        self.assertEqual(response.status_code, 200)
        self.assertEqual(response.get_json(), [])

    def test_create_user(self):
        response = self.client.post('/api/users',
json={'username': 'john', 'email': 'john@example.com'})
        self.assertEqual(response.status_code, 201)
        user = response.get_json()
        self.assertEqual(user['username'], 'john')
        self.assertEqual(user['email'], 'john@example.com')

if __name__ == '__main__':
    unittest.main()
```

8. Running the Application

Activate your virtual environment and install dependencies:

```bash
source venv/bin/activate
pip install -r requirements.txt
```

Run the Flask application:

```bash
```

```
python run.py
```

You can now test your API endpoints using a tool like `curl` or Postman. For example, to create a user:

```bash
curl -X POST http://127.0.0.1:5000/api/users -H "Content-Type: application/json" -d '{"username": "john", "email": "john@example.com"}'
```

To get the list of users:

```bash
curl http://127.0.0.1:5000/api/users
```

9. Running Tests

Run the tests with:

```bash
python -m unittest discover tests
```

This command will discover and run all the tests in the `tests` directory, providing feedback on the success or failure of each test.

A well-structured Flask application lays the foundation for growth, making it easier to maintain and scale as your project evolves. By organizing your code into a clear hierarchy, you ensure that each component has a defined role, which promotes clean coding practices and simplifies debugging and testing. This guide has provided a comprehensive structure and detailed examples to help you build a scalable and maintainable Flask API. As your application grows, this structured approach will support adding new features, integrating with other services, and collaborating with other developers.

Blueprints: Modularizing Your API for Maintainability

Flask, being a micro web framework for Python, is inherently simple yet extremely powerful. One of the core features that make Flask highly maintainable and scalable is Blueprints. Blueprints allow you to break down your application into smaller, modular components, each with its own routes, models, and templates. This modularity promotes cleaner code, easier testing, and better collaboration among developers.

What are Blueprints?

Blueprints in Flask are a way to organize your application into distinct components. Each blueprint can encapsulate routes, templates, static files, and other functionalities. By dividing your application into blueprints, you can keep your codebase manageable, especially as your application grows.

Benefits of Using Blueprints

1. Modularity: Blueprints allow you to divide your application into logical sections, each responsible for specific functionality.

2. Maintainability: Smaller, self-contained modules are easier to maintain, test, and debug.

3. Reusability: Blueprints can be reused across different applications or projects.

4. Collaboration: Different teams can work on different blueprints simultaneously without causing conflicts.

Setting Up Blueprints in Flask

To demonstrate the use of Blueprints, we will build a simple Flask API with user and product management modules. Each module will have its own blueprint.

Project Structure

Here's a suggested structure for a Flask application using Blueprints:

```
my_flask_api/
│
├── venv/
├── app/
│   ├── __init__.py
│   ├── config.py
│   ├── models.py
│   ├── user/
│   │   ├── __init__.py
│   │   ├── routes.py
│   │   └── models.py
│   ├── product/
│   │   ├── __init__.py
│   │   ├── routes.py
│   │   └── models.py
├── tests/
│   ├── __init__.py
│   ├── test_user_routes.py
```

```
│   ├── test_product_routes.py
├── migrations/
│   └── README.md
├── .gitignore
├── requirements.txt
├── run.py
└── README.md
```

Setting Up the Application

1. Initialize the Flask App: Create `app/__init__.py` to initialize the Flask app and register blueprints.

```python
from flask import Flask
from flask_sqlalchemy import SQLAlchemy
from flask_migrate import Migrate

db = SQLAlchemy()
migrate = Migrate()

def create_app():
    app = Flask(__name__)
    app.config.from_object('app.config.Config')

    db.init_app(app)
    migrate.init_app(app, db)
```

```
    from app.user import user_bp
    from app.product import product_bp

    app.register_blueprint(user_bp, url_prefix='/api/users')
    app.register_blueprint(product_bp, url_prefix='/api/products')

    return app
```

2. Configuration Settings: Create `app/config.py` for configuration settings.

```python
import os

class Config:
    SECRET_KEY = os.environ.get('SECRET_KEY', 'default_secret_key')
    SQLALCHEMY_DATABASE_URI = os.environ.get('DATABASE_URL', 'sqlite:///app.db')
    SQLALCHEMY_TRACK_MODIFICATIONS = False
```

3. Database Models: Define your database models in `app/models.py`.

```python
from app import db

class User(db.Model):
    id = db.Column(db.Integer, primary_key=True)
    username = db.Column(db.String(64), unique=True, nullable=False)
    email = db.Column(db.String(120), unique=True, nullable=False)

    def __repr__(self):
        return f'<User {self.username}>'

class Product(db.Model):
    id = db.Column(db.Integer, primary_key=True)
    name = db.Column(db.String(128), nullable=False)
    price = db.Column(db.Float, nullable=False)

    def __repr__(self):
        return f'<Product {self.name}>'
```

Creating User Blueprint

1. Initialize User Blueprint: Create `app/user/__init__.py`.

```python
from flask import Blueprint

user_bp = Blueprint('user', __name__)

from . import routes
```

2. User Routes: Define user-related routes in `app/user/routes.py`.

```python
from flask import request, jsonify
from app import db
from app.models import User
from . import user_bp

@user_bp.route('/', methods=['GET'])
def get_users():
    users = User.query.all()
    return jsonify([{'id': user.id, 'username': user.username, 'email': user.email} for user in users])

@user_bp.route('/', methods=['POST'])
def create_user():
```

```
data = request.get_json()
new_user = User(username=data['username'], email=data['email'])
db.session.add(new_user)
db.session.commit()
return jsonify({'id': new_user.id, 'username': new_user.username, 'email': new_user.email}), 201
```

Creating Product Blueprint

1. Initialize Product Blueprint: Create `app/product/__init__.py`.

```python
from flask import Blueprint

product_bp = Blueprint('product', __name__)

from . import routes
```

2. Product Routes: Define product-related routes in `app/product/routes.py`.

```python
from flask import request, jsonify
from app import db
```

```python
from app.models import Product
from . import product_bp

@product_bp.route('/', methods=['GET'])
def get_products():
    products = Product.query.all()
    return jsonify([{'id': product.id, 'name': product.name, 'price': product.price} for product in products])

@product_bp.route('/', methods=['POST'])
def create_product():
    data = request.get_json()
    new_product = Product(name=data['name'], price=data['price'])
    db.session.add(new_product)
    db.session.commit()
    return jsonify({'id': new_product.id, 'name': new_product.name, 'price': new_product.price}), 201
```

Running the Application

1. Entry Point: Create `run.py` to run the application.

```python
from app import create_app
```

```
app = create_app()

if __name__ == '__main__':
    app.run(debug=True)
```

2. Install Dependencies: Ensure all required packages are listed in `requirements.txt`.

```
Flask
Flask-SQLAlchemy
Flask-Migrate
```

3. Activate Virtual Environment and Install Dependencies:

```bash
source venv/bin/activate
pip install -r requirements.txt
```

4. Run the Application:

```bash
python run.py
```

5. Testing Endpoints:

- **Get users:** `http://127.0.0.1:5000/api/users/`

- **Create user:** Send a POST request to `http://127.0.0.1:5000/api/users/` with a JSON body.

- **Get products:** `http://127.0.0.1:5000/api/products/`

- **Create product:** Send a POST request to `http://127.0.0.1:5000/api/products/` with a JSON body.

Testing with Unit Tests

Testing each blueprint separately ensures that each module works as expected and helps catch bugs early.

1. Initialize Tests: Create `tests/__init__.py`.

```python
# tests/__init__.py
# This file can be empty or contain test initialization code.
```

2. User Routes Tests: Create `tests/test_user_routes.py`.

```python
import unittest
from app import create_app, db
from app.models import User

class UserRoutesTestCase(unittest.TestCase):

    def setUp(self):
        self.app = create_app()
        self.app.config['TESTING'] = True
        self.app.config['SQLALCHEMY_DATABASE_URI'] = 'sqlite:///:memory:'
        self.client = self.app.test_client()

        with self.app.app_context():
            db.create_all()

    def tearDown(self):
        with self.app.app_context():
            db.session.remove()
            db.drop_all()

    def test_get_users(self):
        response = self.client.get('/api/users/')
```

```python
        self.assertEqual(response.status_code, 200)
        self.assertEqual(response.get_json(), [])

    def test_create_user(self):
        response = self.client.post('/api/users/',
json={'username': 'john', 'email': 'john@example.com'})
        self.assertEqual(response.status_code, 201)
        user = response.get_json()
        self.assertEqual(user['username'], 'john')
        self.assertEqual(user['email'],
'john@example.com')

if __name__ == '__main__':
    unittest.main()
```

3. Product Routes Tests: Create `tests/test_product_routes.py`.

```python
import unittest
from app import create_app, db
from app.models import Product

class ProductRoutesTestCase(unittest.TestCase):

    def setUp(self):
        self.app = create_app()
```

```python
        self.app.config['TESTING'] = True
        self.app.config['SQLALCHEMY_DATABASE_URI'] = 'sqlite:///:memory:'
        self.client = self.app.test_client()

        with self.app.app_context():
            db.create_all()

    def tearDown(self):
        with self.app.app_context():
            db.session.remove()
            db.drop_all()

    def test_get_products(self):
        response = self.client.get('/api/products/')
        self.assertEqual(response.status_code, 200)
        self.assertEqual(response.get_json(), [])

    def test_create_product(self):
        response = self.client.post('/api/products/', json={'name': 'Laptop', 'price': 999.99})
        self.assertEqual(response.status_code, 201)
        product = response.get_json()
        self.assertEqual(product['name'], 'Laptop')
        self.assertEqual(product['price'], 999.99)

if __name__ == '__main__':
```

        unittest.main()
    ```

## Running Tests

To ensure your application works as expected, run your tests with the following command:

```bash
python -m unittest discover tests
```

This command will discover and run all the tests in the `tests` directory, providing feedback on the success or failure of each test.

Using Blueprints in Flask provides a structured and modular approach to developing large-scale applications. By organizing your code into logical sections, you enhance maintainability, scalability, and reusability. This approach also simplifies testing and collaboration, making it easier for multiple developers to work on the same project without conflicts.

In this guide, we demonstrated how to set up a Flask application using Blueprints, creating separate modules for user and product management. We covered how to initialize blueprints, define routes, and organize database
```

models. Additionally, we included examples of unit tests to ensure each module works correctly.

As your application grows, you can continue to add new blueprints for different functionalities, keeping your codebase organized and manageable. This modular approach will support the addition of new features, integration with other services, and collaboration with other developers, ensuring the long-term success of your project.

Dependency Injection: Keeping Your Code Clean and Organized

Dependency Injection (DI) is a powerful design pattern that enhances code maintainability, testability, and reusability. It allows you to inject dependencies into a class, rather than the class creating the dependencies itself. This approach decouples the class from its dependencies, making the code more modular and easier to manage. In Python, DI is particularly useful when developing APIs with Flask, a lightweight web framework. This article explores the principles of DI and demonstrates how to implement it in a Flask API.

Understanding Dependency Injection

At its core, DI involves three main components:

1. Client: The class that depends on a service.

2. Service: The class that provides the required functionality.

3. Injector: The code responsible for injecting the service into the client.

The main advantage of DI is that it promotes loose coupling between the client and the service. This makes the system more flexible and easier to maintain.

Why Use Dependency Injection?

1. Improved Testability: DI makes it easier to mock dependencies during unit testing.

2. Enhanced Readability and Maintainability: By separating concerns, DI helps keep code organized and easier to understand.

3. Flexibility and Reusability: DI allows you to swap implementations of dependencies without changing the client code.

Implementing Dependency Injection in Flask

Flask, being a micro-framework, doesn't come with built-in support for DI. However, it is flexible enough to accommodate DI patterns. Let's walk through an example of setting up DI in a Flask API.

Step 1: Setting Up the Flask Application

First, we need to install Flask if we haven't already:

```bash
pip install flask
```

Let's create a basic Flask application:

```python
# app.py
from flask import Flask, jsonify

app = Flask(__name__)

@app.route('/')
def home():
    return jsonify(message="Hello, World!")

if __name__ == "__main__":
    app.run(debug=True)
```

Step 2: Defining Services and Clients

Assume we have a simple service that provides greeting messages. We will create a `GreetingService` class for this purpose.

```python
# services.py
class GreetingService:
    def get_greeting(self) -> str:
        return "Hello, Dependency Injection!"
```

Next, we'll create a client class that depends on the `GreetingService`.

```python
# clients.py
from services import GreetingService

class GreetingClient:
    def __init__(self, greeting_service: GreetingService):
        self.greeting_service = greeting_service

    def greet(self) -> str:
        return self.greeting_service.get_greeting()
```

Step 3: Setting Up the Dependency Injector

We need an injector to manage our dependencies. For simplicity, we can create a basic injector using a function that initializes our dependencies.

```python
# injector.py
from services import GreetingService
from clients import GreetingClient

def configure_injector():
    greeting_service = GreetingService()
    greeting_client = GreetingClient(greeting_service)
    return greeting_client
```

Step 4: Integrating DI with Flask

Now, let's integrate our DI setup with the Flask application. We'll modify our Flask app to use the `GreetingClient` via dependency injection.

```python
# app.py
from flask import Flask, jsonify
from injector import configure_injector
```

```python
app = Flask(__name__)

greeting_client = configure_injector()

@app.route('/')
def home():
    return jsonify(message=greeting_client.greet())

if __name__ == "__main__":
    app.run(debug=True)
```

Step 5: Testing the Application

Run the Flask application:

```bash
python app.py
```

Navigate to `http://127.0.0.1:5000/` in your browser. You should see the following JSON response:

```json
{
    "message": "Hello, Dependency Injection!"
}
```

```

## Advanced Dependency Injection Techniques

While the above example is straightforward, real-world applications often require more sophisticated DI setups. Let's explore a few advanced techniques.

### Using a DI Framework

To manage more complex dependency graphs, you can use a DI framework like `Flask-Injector`.

First, install `Flask-Injector`:

```bash
pip install Flask-Injector
```

Modify the previous example to use `Flask-Injector`:

```python
# app.py
from flask import Flask, jsonify
from flask_injector import FlaskInjector
from injector import inject, singleton, Binder
from services import GreetingService
from clients import GreetingClient
```
```

```python
app = Flask(__name__)

@inject
@app.route('/')
def home(greeting_client: GreetingClient):
    return jsonify(message=greeting_client.greet())

def configure(binder: Binder) -> Binder:
    binder.bind(GreetingService, to=GreetingService, scope=singleton)
    binder.bind(GreetingClient, to=GreetingClient, scope=singleton)

FlaskInjector(app=app, modules=[configure])

if __name__ == "__main__":
    app.run(debug=True)
```
```

## **Dependency Injection in Real-World Scenarios**

In a real-world Flask application, you might have multiple services and clients. Let's consider a more comprehensive example where we have a user service and a notification service.

### **Step 1: Defining the Services**
```

Create a file `services.py`:

```python
# services.py
class UserService:
    def get_user(self, user_id: int) -> dict:
        return {"id": user_id, "name": "John Doe"}

class NotificationService:
    def send_notification(self, message: str) -> str:
        return f"Notification sent: {message}"
```

Step 2: Creating the Client

Create a file `clients.py`:

```python
# clients.py
from services import UserService, NotificationService

class UserClient:
    def __init__(self, user_service: UserService, notification_service: NotificationService):
        self.user_service = user_service
        self.notification_service = notification_service
```

```python
    def get_user_and_notify(self, user_id: int) -> str:
        user = self.user_service.get_user(user_id)
        notification = self.notification_service.send_notification(f"Welcome {user['name']}!")
        return f"User: {user}, {notification}"
```

Step 3: Setting Up the Injector

Create a file `injector.py`:

```python
# injector.py
from services import UserService, NotificationService
from clients import UserClient

def configure_injector():
    user_service = UserService()
    notification_service = NotificationService()
    user_client = UserClient(user_service, notification_service)
    return user_client
```

Step 4: Integrating with Flask

Modify the Flask application to use the new client:

```python
# app.py
from flask import Flask, jsonify
from injector import configure_injector

app = Flask(__name__)

user_client = configure_injector()

@app.route('/user/<int:user_id>')
def get_user(user_id: int):
    return jsonify(message=user_client.get_user_and_notify(user_id))

if __name__ == "__main__":
    app.run(debug=True)
```

Dependency Injection is a crucial design pattern that helps in keeping your code clean, organized, and testable. In the context of Flask API development, it allows you to decouple your components, making your application more modular and maintainable. By using DI, you can easily manage complex dependency graphs and swap implementations without affecting the client code.

In this article, we've covered the basics of DI and demonstrated how to implement it in a Flask application. We started with a simple example and then explored more advanced techniques using `Flask-Injector`. By applying these principles, you can significantly improve the quality and maintainability of your Flask applications.

Configuration Management: Secrets Deserve a Safe Place

Configuration management is a critical aspect of software development, ensuring that application settings, including sensitive information such as API keys, database credentials, and encryption secrets, are handled securely and efficiently. In Python API development with Flask, managing these configurations correctly is essential to maintain both security and ease of deployment. This article delves into the principles of configuration management and demonstrates best practices with practical examples.

Understanding Configuration Management

Configuration management involves organizing and maintaining the state of a system, particularly the configurations and settings that control its behavior. In the context of Flask applications, this includes:

1. Application Settings: General settings such as debug mode, server port, etc.

2. Environment Variables: Variables that differ across environments (development, testing, production).

3. Secrets and Sensitive Information: API keys, database credentials, and other sensitive data that should not be exposed.

Why Proper Configuration Management Matters

1. Security: Protecting sensitive information from unauthorized access.

2. Flexibility: Enabling easy changes in configuration without altering the codebase.

3. Consistency: Ensuring that configurations are consistent across different environments.

4. Maintainability: Simplifying the process of updating and managing configurations.

Implementing Configuration Management in Flask

Step 1: Setting Up a Flask Application

First, we need to install Flask if we haven't already:

```bash
pip install flask
```

Let's create a basic Flask application:

```python
# app.py
from flask import Flask, jsonify
import os

app = Flask(__name__)

@app.route('/')
def home():
    return jsonify(message="Hello, Configuration Management!")

if __name__ == "__main__":
    app.run(debug=True)
```

Step 2: Using Configuration Files

Flask allows you to load configurations from various sources. One common approach is to use a configuration file. Create a `config.py` file to store configurations:

```python
# config.py
import os

class Config:
    DEBUG = False
    TESTING = False
    DATABASE_URI = 'sqlite:///:memory:'
    SECRET_KEY = os.environ.get('SECRET_KEY', 'default-secret-key')

class DevelopmentConfig(Config):
    DEBUG = True
    DATABASE_URI = 'sqlite:///dev.db'

class TestingConfig(Config):
    TESTING = True
    DATABASE_URI = 'sqlite:///test.db'

class ProductionConfig(Config):
    DATABASE_URI = os.environ.get('DATABASE_URI', 'sqlite:///prod.db')
```

Modify the Flask application to use these configurations:

```python
# app.py
from flask import Flask, jsonify
import os

app = Flask(__name__)

# Load configuration from environment variable
config_type = os.getenv('FLASK_CONFIG', 'config.DevelopmentConfig')
app.config.from_object(config_type)

@app.route('/')
def home():
    return jsonify(message="Hello, Configuration Management!", debug=app.config['DEBUG'])

if __name__ == "__main__":
    app.run()
```

To switch between configurations, set the `FLASK_CONFIG` environment variable:

```bash
export FLASK_CONFIG=config.ProductionConfig
```

```
python app.py
```

Step 3: Managing Secrets with Environment Variables

Storing secrets directly in configuration files is a security risk. Instead, use environment variables to manage secrets.

Update your `config.py` to retrieve secrets from environment variables:

```python
# config.py
import os

class Config:
    DEBUG = False
    TESTING = False
    DATABASE_URI = 'sqlite:///:memory:'
    SECRET_KEY = os.environ.get('SECRET_KEY', 'default-secret-key')

class DevelopmentConfig(Config):
    DEBUG = True
    DATABASE_URI = 'sqlite:///dev.db'
```

```
class TestingConfig(Config):
    TESTING = True
    DATABASE_URI = 'sqlite:///test.db'

class ProductionConfig(Config):
    DATABASE_URI = os.environ.get('DATABASE_URI', 'sqlite:///prod.db')
    SECRET_KEY = os.environ.get('SECRET_KEY', 'your-production-secret-key')
```

Set the environment variables before running the application:

```bash
export SECRET_KEY=your-production-secret-key
export DATABASE_URI=your-database-uri
export FLASK_CONFIG=config.ProductionConfig
python app.py
```

Step 4: Using `.env` Files for Local Development

To simplify setting environment variables during local development, you can use a `.env` file along with the `python-dotenv` package.

First, install `python-dotenv`:

```bash
pip install python-dotenv
```

Create a `.env` file in your project root:

```plaintext
# .env
SECRET_KEY=your-development-secret-key
DATABASE_URI=sqlite:///dev.db
FLASK_CONFIG=config.DevelopmentConfig
```

Update `app.py` to load environment variables from the `.env` file:

```python
# app.py
from flask import Flask, jsonify
from dotenv import load_dotenv
import os

load_dotenv()

app = Flask(__name__)
```

```
config_type = os.getenv('FLASK_CONFIG',
'config.DevelopmentConfig')
app.config.from_object(config_type)

@app.route('/')
def home():
    return jsonify(message="Hello, Configuration Management!", debug=app.config['DEBUG'])

if __name__ == "__main__":
    app.run()
```

Step 5: Securely Managing Secrets with AWS Secrets Manager

For production environments, it's best to use a dedicated secrets management service. AWS Secrets Manager is one such service. It allows you to securely store and retrieve secrets.

First, install the AWS SDK for Python, Boto3:

```bash
pip install boto3
```

Assuming you have already stored your secrets in AWS Secrets Manager, update your `config.py` to retrieve secrets from AWS:

```python
# config.py
import os
import boto3
from botocore.exceptions import NoCredentialsError, PartialCredentialsError

class Config:
    DEBUG = False
    TESTING = False
    DATABASE_URI = 'sqlite:///:memory:'
    SECRET_KEY = 'default-secret-key'

    @staticmethod
    def get_secret(secret_name):
        try:
            client = boto3.client('secretsmanager')
            response = client.get_secret_value(SecretId=secret_name)
            return response['SecretString']
        except (NoCredentialsError, PartialCredentialsError):
            return None
```

```
class DevelopmentConfig(Config):
    DEBUG = True
    DATABASE_URI = 'sqlite:///dev.db'

class TestingConfig(Config):
    TESTING = True
    DATABASE_URI = 'sqlite:///test.db'

class ProductionConfig(Config):
    DATABASE_URI = Config.get_secret('prod/DATABASE_URI')
    SECRET_KEY = Config.get_secret('prod/SECRET_KEY')
```

Make sure you have the necessary AWS credentials configured in your environment for this to work.

Step 6: Managing Configuration for Different Environments

In real-world applications, configurations vary between development, testing, and production environments. Flask's configuration system allows you to easily manage these differences.

Example structure of your project:

```
my_flask_app/
│
├── config.py
├── app.py
└── .env
```

Contents of `config.py`:

```python
import os

class Config:
    DEBUG = False
    TESTING = False
    DATABASE_URI = 'sqlite:///:memory:'
    SECRET_KEY = os.getenv('SECRET_KEY', 'default-secret-key')

class DevelopmentConfig(Config):
    DEBUG = True
    DATABASE_URI = os.getenv('DATABASE_URI', 'sqlite:///dev.db')

class TestingConfig(Config):
    TESTING = True
```

```
    DATABASE_URI = os.getenv('DATABASE_URI', 'sqlite:///test.db')

class ProductionConfig(Config):
    DATABASE_URI = os.getenv('DATABASE_URI', 'sqlite:///prod.db')
    SECRET_KEY = os.getenv('SECRET_KEY', 'default-secret-key')
```

Modify `app.py` to load the appropriate configuration based on the environment:

```python
from flask import Flask, jsonify
import os

app = Flask(__name__)

config_type = os.getenv('FLASK_CONFIG', 'config.DevelopmentConfig')
app.config.from_object(config_type)

@app.route('/')
def home():
    return jsonify(message="Hello, Configuration Management!", debug=app.config['DEBUG'])
```

```
if __name__ == "__main__":
    app.run()
```

Proper configuration management is essential for secure, flexible, and maintainable Flask applications. By separating configuration from code, using environment variables for sensitive information, and leveraging tools like `.env` files for local development, you can keep your application settings organized and secure. For production environments, integrating with secrets management services like AWS Secrets Manager ensures that your secrets are stored securely and can be accessed reliably.

In this article, we covered the basics of configuration management and demonstrated how to implement best practices in a Flask application. By following these principles, you can enhance the security and maintainability of your Flask APIs, making them robust and easier to manage across different environments.

Chapter 3

RESTful Design Principles: Building a Consistent and Predictable API

REST (Representational State Transfer) is an architectural style for designing networked applications. It relies on a stateless, client-server communication protocol—usually HTTP. In the context of web APIs, RESTful design principles are crucial for creating a consistent and predictable interface. This article explores these principles and demonstrates their application in Python API development using Flask.

Understanding RESTful Design

RESTful design emphasizes the following principles:

1. Statelessness: Each request from a client to a server must contain all the information needed to understand and process the request.

2. Uniform Interface: Resources are identified in requests using URIs, and the same set of operations is applied to these resources using HTTP methods.

3. Client-Server Architecture: The client and server are separate, allowing each to evolve independently.

4. Cacheability: Responses must define themselves as cacheable or not to prevent clients from reusing stale or inappropriate data.

5. Layered System: A client cannot ordinarily tell whether it is connected directly to the end server or an intermediary along the way.

6. Code on Demand (Optional): Servers can extend client functionality by transferring executable code.

Key Components of a RESTful API

1. Resources and URIs: Resources are the fundamental components of REST, and each resource is identified by a URI.

2. HTTP Methods: RESTful APIs use standard HTTP methods to perform operations on resources.

- `GET`: Retrieve a resource.

- `POST`: Create a new resource.

- `PUT`: Update an existing resource.

- `DELETE`: Remove a resource.

- `PATCH`: Partially update a resource.

3. Statelessness: Each request from a client to a server must contain all the information needed to understand and process the request.

4. Representations: Resources are typically represented in formats such as JSON or XML.

5. Error Handling: Consistent and meaningful error messages should be provided.

6. Hypermedia as the Engine of Application State (HATEOAS): Clients interact with a network application entirely through hypermedia provided dynamically by application servers.

Building a RESTful API with Flask

Flask, a lightweight WSGI web application framework in Python, is well-suited for building RESTful APIs. Let's walk through the process of creating a simple RESTful API with Flask.

Step 1: Setting Up the Flask Application

First, install Flask if you haven't already:

```bash
pip install flask
```

Create a basic Flask application:

```python
# app.py
from flask import Flask, jsonify, request

app = Flask(__name__)

@app.route('/')
def home():
    return jsonify(message="Welcome to the RESTful API")

if __name__ == "__main__":
    app.run(debug=True)
```

Step 2: Defining Resources and Endpoints

Let's define a simple resource, `Book`, with CRUD operations.

Create a file `books.py` to handle the book data:

```python
# books.py
books = []

def get_all_books():
    return books

def get_book(book_id):
    book = next((book for book in books if book['id'] == book_id), None)
    return book

def create_book(data):
    book = {
        'id': data['id'],
        'title': data['title'],
        'author': data['author']
    }
    books.append(book)
    return book

def update_book(book_id, data):
    book = get_book(book_id)
    if book:
        book.update(data)
    return book
```

```
def delete_book(book_id):
    book = get_book(book_id)
    if book:
        books.remove(book)
    return book
```

Step 3: Creating RESTful Endpoints

Update `app.py` to include the endpoints for the `Book` resource:

```python
# app.py
from flask import Flask, jsonify, request, abort
from books import get_all_books, get_book, create_book, update_book, delete_book

app = Flask(__name__)

@app.route('/api/books', methods=['GET'])
def api_get_books():
    return jsonify(get_all_books()), 200

@app.route('/api/books/<int:book_id>', methods=['GET'])
def api_get_book(book_id):
    book = get_book(book_id)
```

```python
    if book is None:
        abort(404)
    return jsonify(book), 200

@app.route('/api/books', methods=['POST'])
def api_create_book():
    if not request.json or not 'id' in request.json:
        abort(400)
    book = create_book(request.json)
    return jsonify(book), 201

@app.route('/api/books/<int:book_id>',
methods=['PUT'])
def api_update_book(book_id):
    if not request.json:
        abort(400)
    book = update_book(book_id, request.json)
    if book is None:
        abort(404)
    return jsonify(book), 200

@app.route('/api/books/<int:book_id>',
methods=['DELETE'])
def api_delete_book(book_id):
    book = delete_book(book_id)
    if book is None:
        abort(404)
    return jsonify({'result': True}), 204
```

```
if __name__ == "__main__":
    app.run(debug=True)
```

Step 4: Implementing Error Handling

Proper error handling is crucial for a RESTful API. Update `app.py` to include custom error handlers:

```python
# app.py
from flask import Flask, jsonify, request, abort
from books import get_all_books, get_book, create_book, update_book, delete_book

app = Flask(__name__)

@app.errorhandler(400)
def bad_request(error):
    return jsonify({'error': 'Bad Request'}), 400

@app.errorhandler(404)
def not_found(error):
    return jsonify({'error': 'Not Found'}), 404

@app.route('/api/books', methods=['GET'])
def api_get_books():
```

```python
    return jsonify(get_all_books()), 200

@app.route('/api/books/<int:book_id>',
methods=['GET'])
def api_get_book(book_id):
    book = get_book(book_id)
    if book is None:
        abort(404)
    return jsonify(book), 200

@app.route('/api/books', methods=['POST'])
def api_create_book():
    if not request.json or not 'id' in request.json:
        abort(400)
    book = create_book(request.json)
    return jsonify(book), 201

@app.route('/api/books/<int:book_id>',
methods=['PUT'])
def api_update_book(book_id):
    if not request.json:
        abort(400)
    book = update_book(book_id, request.json)
    if book is None:
        abort(404)
    return jsonify(book), 200
```

```
@app.route('/api/books/<int:book_id>',
methods=['DELETE'])
def api_delete_book(book_id):
    book = delete_book(book_id)
    if book is None:
        abort(404)
    return jsonify({'result': True}), 204

if __name__ == "__main__":
    app.run(debug=True)
```

Step 5: Ensuring Consistency and Predictability

Consistency and predictability are crucial for a RESTful API. This involves:

1. Using Consistent Naming Conventions: Use nouns for endpoint names and avoid verbs.

2. Returning Appropriate Status Codes: Use the correct HTTP status codes for responses.

3. Providing Meaningful Error Messages: Ensure that error messages are descriptive and helpful.

4. Documenting the API: Provide clear and comprehensive documentation.

Advanced RESTful Design Considerations

Pagination, Filtering, and Sorting

For endpoints that return collections, such as the list of books, it's essential to support pagination, filtering, and sorting.

```python
# books.py
def get_all_books(limit=None, offset=None, sort_by=None, order='asc'):
    books_list = books
    if sort_by:
        reverse = order == 'desc'
        books_list = sorted(books_list, key=lambda x: x[sort_by], reverse=reverse)
    if limit is not None and offset is not None:
        books_list = books_list[offset:offset + limit]
    return books_list
```

Update the `api_get_books` endpoint to handle query parameters:

```python
# app.py
```

```python
@app.route('/api/books', methods=['GET'])
def api_get_books():
    limit = request.args.get('limit', default=None, type=int)
    offset = request.args.get('offset', default=None, type=int)
    sort_by = request.args.get('sort_by', default=None, type=str)
    order = request.args.get('order', default='asc', type=str)
    return jsonify(get_all_books(limit, offset, sort_by, order)), 200
```

Hypermedia as the Engine of Application State (HATEOAS)

HATEOAS ensures that clients interact with the application through links provided by the server, making the API more discoverable.

```python
# books.py
from flask import url_for

def get_all_books():
    return [{'id': book['id'], 'title': book['title'], 'author': book['author'], '_links': {'self': url_for('api_get_book',
```

book_id=book['id'], _external=True)}} for book in books]
```

RESTful design principles are essential for creating APIs that are consistent, predictable, and easy to use. By following these principles, you can ensure that your API is well-structured and maintainable. In this article, we've explored the core principles of RESTful design and demonstrated how to implement them using Flask. We've also covered advanced topics such as pagination, filtering, and HATEOAS to make your API more robust and

## HTTP Methods in Action: Verbs that Power Your API (GET, POST, PUT, DELETE)

HTTP methods, also known as verbs, play a crucial role in defining the actions that can be performed on resources in a RESTful API. Each method has a specific purpose, and understanding when to use each one is essential for designing a robust and intuitive API. In this article, we'll explore the four primary HTTP methods—GET, POST, PUT, and DELETE—and demonstrate their implementation in Python API development using Flask.

### Understanding HTTP Methods
```

1. GET: Used to retrieve data from a server. GET requests should only retrieve data and should not modify the server's state.

2. POST: Used to submit data to be processed to a specified resource. It often results in the creation of a new resource or the updating of an existing one.

3. PUT: Used to update an existing resource or create a new one if it does not exist. PUT requests are idempotent, meaning that making the same request multiple times will have the same effect as making it once.

4. DELETE: Used to delete a resource identified by the specified URI.

Building a Flask API with HTTP Methods

Let's walk through the process of implementing each of these HTTP methods in a Flask API.

Step 1: Setting Up the Flask Application

First, install Flask if you haven't already:

```bash
pip install flask
```

```

Create a basic Flask application:

```python
# app.py
from flask import Flask, jsonify, request

app = Flask(__name__)

if __name__ == "__main__":
    app.run(debug=True)
```

Step 2: Implementing the GET Method

The GET method is used to retrieve data from the server. Let's create an endpoint that returns a list of books.

```python
# app.py
books = [
    {'id': 1, 'title': 'Book 1', 'author': 'Author 1'},
    {'id': 2, 'title': 'Book 2', 'author': 'Author 2'}
]

@app.route('/api/books', methods=['GET'])
def get_books():
```
```

```
    return jsonify(books), 200
```

Step 3: Implementing the POST Method

The POST method is used to submit data to be processed to a specified resource. Let's create an endpoint to add a new book to the list.

```python
# app.py
@app.route('/api/books', methods=['POST'])
def add_book():
    data = request.json
    if 'title' not in data or 'author' not in data:
        return jsonify({'error': 'Title and author are required fields'}), 400
    new_book = {'id': len(books) + 1, 'title': data['title'], 'author': data['author']}
    books.append(new_book)
    return jsonify(new_book), 201
```

Step 4: Implementing the PUT Method

The PUT method is used to update an existing resource or create a new one if it does not exist. Let's create an endpoint to update a book's information.

```python
# app.py
@app.route('/api/books/<int:book_id>', methods=['PUT'])
def update_book(book_id):
    data = request.json
    for book in books:
        if book['id'] == book_id:
            book.update(data)
            return jsonify(book), 200
    return jsonify({'error': 'Book not found'}), 404
```

Step 5: Implementing the DELETE Method

The DELETE method is used to delete a resource identified by the specified URI. Let's create an endpoint to delete a book from the list.

```python
# app.py
@app.route('/api/books/<int:book_id>', methods=['DELETE'])
def delete_book(book_id):
    for i, book in enumerate(books):
        if book['id'] == book_id:
            del books[i]
```

```
        return jsonify({'result': True}), 200
    return jsonify({'error': 'Book not found'}), 404
```

Testing the API

Now that we've implemented the CRUD (Create, Read, Update, Delete) operations using HTTP methods, let's test our API using a REST client like Postman or cURL.

1. GET Request: Retrieve all books

```http
GET /api/books
```

2. POST Request: Add a new book

```http
POST /api/books
Content-Type: application/json

{
   "title": "New Book",
   "author": "New Author"
}
```

3. PUT Request: Update an existing book

```http
PUT /api/books/1
Content-Type: application/json

{
  "title": "Updated Book Title",
  "author": "Updated Author Name"
}
```

4. DELETE Request: Delete a book

```http
DELETE /api/books/1
```

HTTP methods are fundamental building blocks for designing RESTful APIs. By understanding the purpose of each method and how to implement them in a Flask application, you can create powerful and intuitive APIs that interact seamlessly with clients. In this article, we've explored the GET, POST, PUT, and DELETE methods and demonstrated their implementation in a Python API using Flask. With these tools, you can build robust and scalable APIs that meet the needs of your application and its users.

Resource-Oriented Design: Structuring Endpoints Around Your Data

Resource-oriented design is a fundamental approach to structuring RESTful APIs. It revolves around identifying and organizing resources in a way that reflects the data model of your application. By aligning endpoints with the underlying data model, you create an intuitive and consistent API that is easy to understand and use. In this article, we'll delve into the principles of resource-oriented design and demonstrate its implementation in Python API development using Flask.

Understanding Resource-Oriented Design

Resource-oriented design focuses on identifying and modeling resources within an application. A resource is anything that can be uniquely identified and manipulated, such as a user, product, or transaction. Each resource is represented by a URI, and interactions with the API are performed through HTTP methods.

Key principles of resource-oriented design include:

1. Identification: Resources are identified by URIs, which should be hierarchical and meaningful.

2. Representation: Resources are represented in formats such as JSON or XML.

3. Manipulation: Interactions with resources are performed using standard HTTP methods (GET, POST, PUT, DELETE).

4. Statelessness: Each request from a client to a server must contain all the information needed to understand and process the request.

Structuring Endpoints Around Resources

When designing an API, it's essential to identify the resources that your application manages and structure endpoints around them. Let's explore how to implement resource-oriented design in a Flask API.

Step 1: Setting Up the Flask Application

First, install Flask if you haven't already:

```bash
pip install flask
```

Create a basic Flask application:

```python
# app.py
from flask import Flask

app = Flask(__name__)

if __name__ == "__main__":
    app.run(debug=True)
```

Step 2: Defining Resources and Endpoints

Identify the resources in your application and create endpoints to interact with them. For example, let's consider a simple bookstore application with the following resources: `books`, `authors`, and `publishers`.

```python
# app.py
from flask import Flask, jsonify

app = Flask(__name__)

books = [
    {'id': 1, 'title': 'Book 1', 'author': 'Author 1', 'publisher': 'Publisher 1'},
    {'id': 2, 'title': 'Book 2', 'author': 'Author 2', 'publisher': 'Publisher 2'}
```

```python
]

authors = [
    {'id': 1, 'name': 'Author 1'},
    {'id': 2, 'name': 'Author 2'}
]

publishers = [
    {'id': 1, 'name': 'Publisher 1'},
    {'id': 2, 'name': 'Publisher 2'}
]

@app.route('/api/books', methods=['GET'])
def get_books():
    return jsonify(books), 200

@app.route('/api/authors', methods=['GET'])
def get_authors():
    return jsonify(authors), 200

@app.route('/api/publishers', methods=['GET'])
def get_publishers():
    return jsonify(publishers), 200

if __name__ == "__main__":
    app.run(debug=True)
```
```
```

Step 3: Implementing CRUD Operations

Next, implement CRUD (Create, Read, Update, Delete) operations for each resource using appropriate HTTP methods.

```python
# app.py
from flask import Flask, jsonify, request, abort

app = Flask(__name__)

books = [
    {'id': 1, 'title': 'Book 1', 'author': 'Author 1', 'publisher': 'Publisher 1'},
    {'id': 2, 'title': 'Book 2', 'author': 'Author 2', 'publisher': 'Publisher 2'}
]

# GET all books
@app.route('/api/books', methods=['GET'])
def get_books():
    return jsonify(books), 200

# GET a single book by ID
@app.route('/api/books/<int:book_id>', methods=['GET'])
def get_book(book_id):
```

```
    book = next((book for book in books if book['id'] ==
book_id), None)
    if book is None:
        abort(404)
    return jsonify(book), 200

# POST a new book
@app.route('/api/books', methods=['POST'])
def add_book():
    data = request.json
    if 'title' not in data or 'author' not in data or 'publisher'
not in data:
        abort(400)
    new_book = {'id': len(books) + 1, 'title': data['title'],
'author': data['author'], 'publisher': data['publisher']}
    books.append(new_book)
    return jsonify(new_book), 201

# PUT (update) an existing book
@app.route('/api/books/<int:book_id>',
methods=['PUT'])
def update_book(book_id):
    data = request.json
    book = next((book for book in books if book['id'] ==
book_id), None)
    if book is None:
        abort(404)
    book.update(data)
```

```
    return jsonify(book), 200

# DELETE a book by ID
@app.route('/api/books/<int:book_id>',
methods=['DELETE'])
def delete_book(book_id):
    book = next((book for book in books if book['id'] ==
book_id), None)
    if book is None:
        abort(404)
    books.remove(book)
    return jsonify({'result': True}), 204

if __name__ == "__main__":
    app.run(debug=True)
```

Testing the API

Now that we've implemented CRUD operations for our resources, let's test the API using a REST client like Postman or cURL.

1. GET Request: Retrieve all books

```http
GET /api/books
```

2. GET Request: Retrieve a single book by ID

```http
GET /api/books/1
```

3. POST Request: Add a new book

```http
POST /api/books
Content-Type: application/json

{
   "title": "New Book",
   "author": "New Author",
   "publisher": "New Publisher"
}
```

4. PUT Request: Update an existing book

```http
PUT /api/books/1
Content-Type: application/json

{
   "title": "Updated Book Title",
```

```
    "author": "Updated Author Name",
    "publisher": "Updated Publisher Name"
}
```

5. DELETE Request: Delete a book by ID

```http
DELETE /api/books/1
```

Resource-oriented design is a powerful approach to structuring RESTful APIs that emphasizes identifying and organizing resources based on the underlying data model of your application. By aligning endpoints with resources, you create an intuitive and consistent API that is easy to understand and use. In this article, we've explored the principles of resource-oriented design and demonstrated its implementation in Python API development using Flask. By following these principles, you can build robust and scalable APIs that effectively expose your application's data to clients.

Versioning Your API: Ensuring Smooth Transitions and Backward Compatibility

Versioning your API is crucial for maintaining compatibility and providing a smooth transition for clients when making changes or introducing new features. By versioning your API, you can ensure that existing clients continue to function as expected while allowing new clients to take advantage of updated functionality. In this article, we'll explore the importance of versioning, different versioning strategies, and how to implement versioning in Python API development using Flask.

Why Version Your API?

Versioning your API offers several benefits:

1. Backward Compatibility: Allows existing clients to continue functioning without disruption when changes are made to the API.

2. Smooth Transition: Provides a clear path for clients to migrate to newer versions of the API.

3. Feature Rollouts: Enables the introduction of new features and improvements without impacting existing clients.

4. Client Isolation: Allows different versions of the API to coexist, enabling clients to choose the version that best suits their needs.

Versioning Strategies

There are several strategies for versioning an API:

1. URL Versioning: Version information is included in the URL path.

2. Header Versioning: Version information is included in a custom HTTP header.

3. Query Parameter Versioning: Version information is included as a query parameter in the URL.

4. Media Type Versioning: Version information is included in the media type (e.g., `application/vnd.company.v1+json`).

Each strategy has its advantages and trade-offs, and the choice depends on factors such as API complexity, client requirements, and personal preference.

Implementing Versioning in Flask

Let's walk through the process of implementing URL versioning in a Flask API.

Step 1: Setting Up the Flask Application

First, install Flask if you haven't already:

```bash
pip install flask
```

Create a basic Flask application:

```python
# app.py
from flask import Flask

app = Flask(__name__)

if __name__ == "__main__":
    app.run(debug=True)
```

Step 2: Implementing URL Versioning

We'll use URL versioning by prefixing all endpoints with the version number in the URL path.

```python
# app.py
from flask import Flask, jsonify

app = Flask(__name__)
```

```
books_v1 = [
    {'id': 1, 'title': 'Book 1', 'author': 'Author 1'},
    {'id': 2, 'title': 'Book 2', 'author': 'Author 2'}
]

books_v2 = [
    {'id': 1, 'title': 'Book 1', 'author': 'Author 1', 'year': 2022},
    {'id': 2, 'title': 'Book 2', 'author': 'Author 2', 'year': 2023}
]

@app.route('/api/v1/books', methods=['GET'])
def get_books_v1():
    return jsonify(books_v1), 200

@app.route('/api/v2/books', methods=['GET'])
def get_books_v2():
    return jsonify(books_v2), 200

if __name__ == "__main__":
    app.run(debug=True)
```

In this example, we have two versions of the `/books` endpoint: `/api/v1/books` and `/api/v2/books`. Clients can choose which version to use by specifying the appropriate URL path.

Testing the API

To test the API, you can use a web browser or a tool like cURL to send requests to the different endpoints.

1. GET Request: Retrieve books from version 1 of the API

```http
GET /api/v1/books
```

2. GET Request: Retrieve books from version 2 of the API

```http
GET /api/v2/books
```

Versioning your API is essential for maintaining compatibility and providing a smooth transition for clients when making changes or introducing new features. By choosing a versioning strategy that aligns with your API's needs and implementing it effectively, you can ensure that your API remains flexible and accessible to both existing and future clients. In this article, we explored the importance of versioning, different versioning strategies, and how to implement versioning in Python API development using Flask. By following these best practices, you can build robust and scalable APIs that meet the evolving needs of your users and stakeholders.

Chapter 4

Working with Data: From Simple Variables to Databases with SQLAlchemy

Working with data is a fundamental aspect of building APIs, from handling simple variables to storing and retrieving data from databases. SQLAlchemy is a powerful toolkit and Object-Relational Mapping (ORM) library for Python that provides an elegant and expressive way to interact with databases. In this article, we'll explore how to work with data in Python API development using Flask and SQLAlchemy, covering everything from managing simple variables to integrating with databases.

Managing Simple Variables

Let's start by creating a Flask application that handles simple variables. We'll create endpoints to retrieve and update these variables.

Step 1: Setting Up the Flask Application

First, install Flask if you haven't already:

```bash
pip install flask
```

```

Create a basic Flask application:

```python
# app.py
from flask import Flask, jsonify, request

app = Flask(__name__)

if __name__ == "__main__":
    app.run(debug=True)
```

Step 2: Implementing Endpoints for Simple Variables

We'll define two simple variables, `name` and `age`, and create endpoints to retrieve and update them.

```python
# app.py
name = "John Doe"
age = 30

@app.route('/api/name', methods=['GET'])
def get_name():
    return jsonify({'name': name}), 200
```
```

```
@app.route('/api/age', methods=['GET'])
def get_age():
    return jsonify({'age': age}), 200

@app.route('/api/update', methods=['POST'])
def update_variables():
    data = request.json
    global name, age
    name = data.get('name', name)
    age = data.get('age', age)
    return jsonify({'message': 'Variables updated successfully'}), 200
```

Now, you can retrieve and update the variables `name` and `age` using the defined endpoints.

Integrating with Databases Using SQLAlchemy

Next, let's integrate SQLAlchemy into our Flask application to work with databases. We'll use SQLite as the database engine for simplicity, but SQLAlchemy supports various database backends.

Step 1: Installing SQLAlchemy

Install SQLAlchemy using pip:

```bash
pip install sqlalchemy
```

Step 2: Defining a Database Model

We'll define a simple database model for storing user information, including their name and age.

```python
# models.py
from sqlalchemy import Column, Integer, String
from sqlalchemy.ext.declarative import declarative_base

Base = declarative_base()

class User(Base):
    __tablename__ = 'users'
    id = Column(Integer, primary_key=True)
    name = Column(String)
    age = Column(Integer)

    def __repr__(self):
        return f"<User(name='{self.name}', age='{self.age}')>"
```

Step 3: Setting Up the Database Connection

Configure the database connection in the Flask application.

```python
# app.py
from flask import Flask
from sqlalchemy import create_engine
from sqlalchemy.orm import sessionmaker
from models import Base, User

app = Flask(__name__)
engine = create_engine('sqlite:///database.db')
Base.metadata.create_all(engine)
Session = sessionmaker(bind=engine)

if __name__ == "__main__":
    app.run(debug=True)
```

Step 4: Implementing Endpoints for Database Operations

We'll create endpoints to perform CRUD (Create, Read, Update, Delete) operations on the `User` model.

```python
# app.py
```

```python
from flask import jsonify, request
from models import User, Session

session = Session()

@app.route('/api/users', methods=['GET'])
def get_users():
    users = session.query(User).all()
    return jsonify([user.__dict__ for user in users]), 200

@app.route('/api/users/<int:user_id>', methods=['GET'])
def get_user(user_id):
    user = session.query(User).filter_by(id=user_id).first()
    if user is None:
        return jsonify({'error': 'User not found'}), 404
    return jsonify(user.__dict__), 200

@app.route('/api/users', methods=['POST'])
def create_user():
    data = request.json
    if 'name' not in data or 'age' not in data:
        return jsonify({'error': 'Name and age are required'}), 400
    user = User(name=data['name'], age=data['age'])
    session.add(user)
    session.commit()
    return jsonify({'message': 'User created successfully'}), 201
```

```
@app.route('/api/users/<int:user_id>', methods=['PUT'])
def update_user(user_id):
    data = request.json
    user = session.query(User).filter_by(id=user_id).first()
    if user is None:
        return jsonify({'error': 'User not found'}), 404
    user.name = data.get('name', user.name)
    user.age = data.get('age', user.age)
    session.commit()
    return jsonify({'message': 'User updated successfully'}), 200

@app.route('/api/users/<int:user_id>', methods=['DELETE'])
def delete_user(user_id):
    user = session.query(User).filter_by(id=user_id).first()
    if user is None:
        return jsonify({'error': 'User not found'}), 404
    session.delete(user)
    session.commit()
    return jsonify({'message': 'User deleted successfully'}), 204
```

Testing the API

Now, you can test the API endpoints using tools like cURL or Postman to interact with the database and perform CRUD operations on the `User` model.

In this article, we explored how to work with data in Python API development using Flask and SQLAlchemy. We started by managing simple variables and creating endpoints to retrieve and update them. Then, we integrated SQLAlchemy to work with databases, defined a database model, set up the database connection, and implemented endpoints for CRUD operations on the database model. By following these steps, you can effectively work with data in your Flask APIs, from handling simple variables to interacting with databases.

Data Validation: Ensuring Your API Receives Clean Information

Data validation is a critical aspect of API development, ensuring that the information received by your API is accurate, consistent, and safe to process. By validating incoming data, you can prevent errors, vulnerabilities, and unexpected behavior in your application. In this article, we'll explore the importance of data validation, common validation techniques, and how to implement data validation in Python API development using Flask.

Importance of Data Validation

Data validation serves several important purposes:

1. Data Integrity: Ensures that data meets specified criteria, preventing inconsistencies and inaccuracies.

2. Security: Protects against malicious input, such as SQL injection, cross-site scripting (XSS), and other security vulnerabilities.

3. Error Handling: Detects and handles errors early in the process, improving the reliability and stability of your application.

4. User Experience: Provides feedback to users about invalid data, guiding them to correct their input and enhancing the user experience.

Common Data Validation Techniques

There are several techniques for validating data in an API:

1. Schema Validation: Defines a schema that describes the structure and constraints of the incoming data.

2. Input Sanitization: Cleans input data by removing or escaping potentially harmful characters and content.

3. Data Type Validation: Checks that data values match the expected data types (e.g., string, integer, boolean).

4. Range and Length Checks: Verifies that data falls within specified ranges or lengths.

5. Regular Expressions: Validates text input against predefined patterns or regular expressions.

6. Whitelisting and Blacklisting: Allows or blocks specific values based on predefined lists.

7. Dependency Validation: Ensures that dependent data fields are consistent and coherent.

Implementing Data Validation in Flask

Let's walk through the process of implementing data validation in a Flask API using some of these techniques.

Step 1: Setting Up the Flask Application

First, install Flask if you haven't already:

```bash
pip install flask
```

Create a basic Flask application:

```python
# app.py
from flask import Flask, jsonify, request

app = Flask(__name__)

if __name__ == "__main__":
    app.run(debug=True)
```

Step 2: Implementing Data Validation Endpoints

We'll create endpoints to demonstrate different data validation techniques.

```python
# app.py
@app.route('/api/validate', methods=['POST'])
def validate_data():
    data = request.json

    # Schema Validation
    if 'name' not in data or 'age' not in data:
        return jsonify({'error': 'Name and age are required fields'}), 400
```

```
# Input Sanitization (No specific example in this code snippet)

# Data Type Validation
if not isinstance(data.get('age'), int):
    return jsonify({'error': 'Age must be an integer'}), 400

# Range and Length Checks
if not 0 < data.get('age') <= 150:
    return jsonify({'error': 'Age must be between 1 and 150'}), 400

# Regular Expressions (No specific example in this code snippet)

# Whitelisting and Blacklisting (No specific example in this code snippet)

# Dependency Validation (No specific example in this code snippet)

return jsonify({'message': 'Data validated successfully'}), 200
```

Testing the API

You can test the API using a tool like cURL or Postman by sending requests with different sets of data and observing the responses.

Data validation is a critical aspect of API development, ensuring that the information received by your API is accurate, consistent, and safe to process. By implementing data validation techniques such as schema validation, input sanitization, data type validation, and others, you can improve the reliability, security, and user experience of your API. In this article, we explored the importance of data validation, common validation techniques, and how to implement data validation in Python API development using Flask. By following these best practices, you can build robust and secure APIs that handle data effectively and prevent potential vulnerabilities and errors.

Serialization: Transforming Data for Seamless Consumption by Clients

Serialization is the process of converting complex data structures into a format that can be easily transmitted and reconstructed by clients. In the context of API development, serialization involves converting Python objects or database records into formats such as JSON or XML, which can be transferred over the network and consumed by clients. Flask provides various tools and libraries to facilitate serialization, making it easier to build APIs that communicate effectively with clients. In this article, we'll explore the importance of serialization, common serialization techniques, and how to implement serialization in Python API development using Flask.

Importance of Serialization

Serialization plays a crucial role in API development for several reasons:

1. Interoperability: Allows APIs to communicate with clients written in different programming languages and running on different platforms.

2. Efficiency: Reduces the size of data transmitted over the network, improving performance and reducing bandwidth usage.

3. Simplicity: Simplifies the process of parsing and processing data on the client side by providing a standardized format.

4. Flexibility: Enables APIs to support multiple data formats, allowing clients to choose the format that best suits their needs.

Common Serialization Techniques

There are several serialization techniques commonly used in API development:

1. JSON Serialization: Converts Python objects or data structures into JSON (JavaScript Object Notation) format, which is widely supported and easy to parse.

2. XML Serialization: Converts data into XML (eXtensible Markup Language) format, which is hierarchical and extensible but less human-readable than JSON.

3. Custom Serialization: Allows developers to define custom serialization methods for specific data types or formats.

4. Serialization Libraries: Utilizes serialization libraries such as `json` or `pickle` in Python to automate the serialization process.

Implementing Serialization in Flask

Let's walk through the process of implementing serialization in a Flask API using JSON serialization as an example.

Step 1: Setting Up the Flask Application

First, install Flask if you haven't already:

```bash
pip install flask
```

Create a basic Flask application:

```python
# app.py
from flask import Flask, jsonify

app = Flask(__name__)

if __name__ == "__main__":
    app.run(debug=True)
```

Step 2: Implementing Serialization Endpoints

We'll create endpoints to demonstrate JSON serialization by returning Python dictionaries as JSON responses.

```python
# app.py
@app.route('/api/user', methods=['GET'])
def get_user():
    user = {'id': 1, 'name': 'John Doe', 'age': 30}
```

```
    return jsonify(user), 200

@app.route('/api/users', methods=['GET'])
def get_users():
    users = [
        {'id': 1, 'name': 'John Doe', 'age': 30},
        {'id': 2, 'name': 'Jane Smith', 'age': 25}
    ]
    return jsonify(users), 200
```

Testing the API

You can test the API by sending requests to the defined endpoints using tools like cURL or Postman. The responses should be in JSON format, demonstrating the serialization process.

Serialization is a critical aspect of API development, enabling APIs to communicate effectively with clients by converting complex data structures into a format that can be easily transmitted and reconstructed. By implementing serialization techniques such as JSON serialization in Python API development using Flask, you can build APIs that are interoperable, efficient, and flexible. In this article, we explored the importance of serialization, common serialization techniques, and how to implement serialization in Flask. By following these best practices, you can create robust and scalable APIs that seamlessly exchange data with clients in a standardized format.

Common Data Formats: JSON, XML, and Beyond

Data formats are essential in API development as they determine how data is structured, transmitted, and consumed by clients. JSON (JavaScript Object Notation) and XML (eXtensible Markup Language) are two widely used data formats in API development due to their simplicity, flexibility, and widespread support. However, there are other emerging data formats worth considering. In this article, we'll explore JSON, XML, and touch upon emerging formats, demonstrating how to work with them in Python API development with Flask.

JSON (JavaScript Object Notation)

JSON is a lightweight, human-readable data interchange format commonly used in web development and API communication. It is based on a subset of the JavaScript programming language, making it easy to parse and manipulate in JavaScript-based applications. JSON data is represented as key-value pairs and supports various data types, including strings, numbers, booleans, arrays, and objects.

Characteristics of JSON:

- **Simple Syntax:** JSON has a straightforward syntax consisting of key-value pairs separated by commas and enclosed in curly braces `{}`.

- **Lightweight**: JSON is lightweight and compact, making it efficient for transmitting data over the network.

- **Human-Readable:** JSON data is easy for humans to read and write, facilitating debugging and troubleshooting.

- **Platform-Independent:** JSON is language-agnostic and supported by most programming languages and platforms.

- **Flexible Data Types:** JSON supports various data types, including strings, numbers, booleans, arrays, objects, and null values.

Use Cases of JSON:

- **API Communication:** JSON is commonly used for transmitting data between clients and servers in API communication.

- **Configuration Files:** JSON is used for storing configuration settings and preferences in web applications and services.

- **Data Exchange:** JSON is used for exchanging data between different systems and applications, such as web services and microservices.

- **Serialization**: JSON is used for serializing complex data structures into a format that can be easily transmitted and reconstructed.

Advantages of JSON:

- **Simplicity**: JSON has a simple and intuitive syntax that is easy to understand and work with.

- **Widespread Support:** JSON is supported by most programming languages, platforms, and libraries, making it highly interoperable.

- **Efficiency**: JSON data is lightweight and compact, reducing bandwidth usage and improving performance.

- **Human-Readable:** JSON data is human-readable and easy to parse, debug, and troubleshoot.

- **Flexibility**: JSON supports various data types and structures, allowing for the representation of complex data.

Disadvantages of JSON:

- **Limited Data Types:** JSON has limited support for complex data types such as dates, binary data, and custom objects.

- **No Schema Validation:** JSON does not provide built-in support for schema validation, making it challenging to enforce data constraints and integrity.

- **Verbose**: JSON data can become verbose and repetitive, especially for nested structures with multiple levels of indentation.

- **Security Concerns:** JSON is susceptible to security vulnerabilities such as JSON injection and data tampering if not properly sanitized and validated.

XML (eXtensible Markup Language)

XML is a markup language designed for storing and transporting data in a hierarchical and structured format. It is widely used in web development, document management, and data exchange due to its extensibility, flexibility, and compatibility with existing systems. XML documents consist of elements, attributes, and text enclosed in tags, allowing for the representation of complex data structures and metadata.

Characteristics of XML:

- **Hierarchical Structure:** XML documents are organized in a hierarchical structure with nested elements representing parent-child relationships.

- **Extensibility**: XML is extensible and allows developers to define custom tags, attributes, and document structures to suit specific requirements.

- **Well-Defined Syntax:** XML has a well-defined syntax consisting of elements, attributes, and text enclosed in angle brackets '< >'.

- **Schema Validation:** XML supports schema validation through Document Type Definitions (DTD) and XML Schema Definition (XSD), allowing for the enforcement of data constraints and integrity.

- **Platform-Independent:** XML is platform-independent and supported by most programming languages, platforms, and libraries.

Use Cases of XML:

- **Document Management:** XML is commonly used for storing and organizing structured documents, such as technical specifications, legal contracts, and financial reports.

- **Data Exchange:** XML is used for exchanging data between different systems and applications, such as web services, databases, and enterprise systems.

- **Configuration Files:** XML is used for storing configuration settings and preferences in software applications and services.

- **Markup Language:** XML is used as a markup language for defining document structures, formatting, and styling in web development and content management.

Advantages of XML:

- **Structure**: XML provides a hierarchical and structured format for representing complex data, making it suitable for a wide range of applications.

- **Extensibility**: XML is extensible and allows developers to define custom tags, attributes, and document structures to meet specific requirements.

- **Schema Validation:** XML supports schema validation, allowing for the enforcement of data constraints and integrity through DTD and XSD.

- **Compatibility**: XML is supported by most programming languages, platforms, and libraries, making it highly interoperable.

- **Legacy Support:** XML has been widely adopted and is compatible with existing systems, databases, and standards.

Disadvantages of XML:

- **Verbosity**: XML documents can become verbose and repetitive, especially for complex data structures with multiple levels of nesting.

- **Complexity**: XML syntax can be more complex and verbose compared to other data formats such as JSON, making it less human-readable and intuitive.

- **Performance Overhead:** XML processing can incur performance overhead, especially for large documents and complex parsing operations.

- **Security Concerns:** XML is susceptible to security vulnerabilities such as XML injection and denial-of-service attacks if not properly sanitized and validated.

Working with JSON and XML in Flask

Flask provides built-in support for working with JSON and XML data formats through its request and response objects. Let's explore how to work with them in a Flask API.

JSON Handling in Flask:

Flask provides the `jsonify` function to convert Python objects into JSON responses. Here's an example of how to use JSON in Flask:

```
```python

```python
from flask import Flask, jsonify

app = Flask(__name__)

@app.route('/api/json', methods=['GET'])
def get_json():
    data = {'name': 'John', 'age': 30}
    return jsonify(data)
```

In this example, the `jsonify` function converts the Python dictionary `data` into a JSON response, which can be consumed by clients.

XML Handling in Flask:

Flask does not have built-in support for XML, but you can use third-party libraries such as `xmltodict` or `xml.etree.ElementTree` to work with XML data. Here's an example using `xmltodict`:

First, install the `xmltodict` library:

```bash
pip install xmltodict
```

Then, you can use it in your Flask application:

```python
from flask import Flask, Response
import xmltodict

app = Flask(__name__)

@app.route('/api/xml', methods=['GET'])
def get_xml():
    data = {'name': 'John', 'age': 30}
    xml_data = xmltodict.unparse({'data': data}, pretty=True)
    return Response(xml_data, mimetype='text/xml')
```

In this example, `xmltodict.unparse` converts the Python dictionary `data` into an XML string, which is then returned as a response with the `text/xml` mimetype.

Beyond JSON and XML: Other Data Formats

While JSON and XML are widely used, there are other emerging data formats worth considering in API development. Some of these formats include:

- **Protocol Buffers:** Protocol Buffers is a binary serialization format developed by Google for efficient data transmission and storage. It offers smaller message sizes and faster serialization/deserialization compared to JSON and XML.

- **MessagePack**: MessagePack is a binary serialization format that is similar to JSON but more compact and efficient. It is suitable for environments where bandwidth and processing power are limited.

- **YAML (YAML Ain't Markup Language)**: YAML is a human-readable data serialization format that is often used for configuration files and data exchange. It offers a more expressive and readable syntax compared to JSON and XML.

- **CSV (Comma-Separated Values)**: CSV is a simple and widely used format for storing tabular data in plain text. It is commonly used for data interchange between spreadsheets and databases.

In this article, we explored the common data formats JSON and XML, discussing their characteristics, use cases, advantages, and disadvantages. We also demonstrated how to work with JSON and XML in Python API development using Flask, including handling JSON responses and converting Python objects to XML. Additionally, we briefly touched upon other emerging data formats such as Protocol Buffers, MessagePack, YAML, and CSV, highlighting their potential applications in API development. By understanding these data formats and their features, you can make informed decisions when designing and implementing APIs that effectively communicate and exchange data with clients.

Chapter 5

Understanding Authentication Mechanisms: Basic, Token-Based, and More

Authentication is a crucial aspect of any web application, ensuring that users are who they claim to be before granting access to resources or functionalities. In this guide, we'll explore various authentication mechanisms, including Basic Authentication, Token-Based Authentication, and more, using Python API development with Flask.

Basic Authentication:

Basic Authentication is one of the simplest authentication mechanisms where the user's credentials (username and password) are sent over HTTP headers. While easy to implement, it's not very secure since credentials are transmitted in plaintext.

Let's implement Basic Authentication in Flask:

```python
from flask import Flask, request, Response

app = Flask(__name__)
```

```python
# User credentials dictionary (for demonstration purposes)
users = {
    "user1": "password1",
    "user2": "password2"
}

@app.route('/login', methods=['POST'])
def login():
    auth = request.authorization
    if auth and auth.username in users and users[auth.username] == auth.password:
        return Response("Login successful", 200)
    else:
        return Response("Invalid credentials", 401)

if __name__ == '__main__':
    app.run(debug=True)
```

Token-Based Authentication:

Token-Based Authentication is widely used in modern web applications. Instead of transmitting credentials with each request, a token is generated upon successful login and sent to the client. The client then includes this token in subsequent requests.

Let's implement Token-Based Authentication in Flask using JWT (JSON Web Tokens):

```python
from flask import Flask, request, jsonify
import jwt
import datetime

app = Flask(__name__)
app.config['SECRET_KEY'] = 'your_secret_key'

# User credentials dictionary (for demonstration purposes)
users = {
   "user1": "password1",
   "user2": "password2"
}

@app.route('/login', methods=['POST'])
def login():
   auth = request.authorization
   if auth and auth.username in users and users[auth.username] == auth.password:
      token = jwt.encode({'user': auth.username, 'exp': datetime.datetime.utcnow() + datetime.timedelta(minutes=30)}, app.config['SECRET_KEY'])
      return jsonify({'token': token.decode('UTF-8')})
```

```
    else:
        return jsonify({'message': 'Invalid credentials'}), 401

@app.route('/protected', methods=['GET'])
def protected():
    token = request.headers.get('Authorization')
    if not token:
        return jsonify({'message': 'Token is missing'}), 401

    try:
        data = jwt.decode(token, app.config['SECRET_KEY'])
        return jsonify({'message': 'Access granted for user: {}'.format(data['user'])}), 200
    except:
        return jsonify({'message': 'Token is invalid'}), 401

if __name__ == '__main__':
    app.run(debug=True)
```

In this implementation, upon successful login, a JWT token is generated containing the user's information and expiration time. This token is then sent to the client, who includes it in subsequent requests. The server verifies the token to grant access to protected resources.

Other Authentication Mechanisms:

Beyond Basic and Token-Based Authentication, there are several other authentication mechanisms worth considering, depending on the application's requirements:

1. OAuth: A protocol allowing third-party services to perform actions on behalf of a user without accessing their credentials directly. It's commonly used for social login and API authorization.

2. OpenID Connect: Built on top of OAuth 2.0, it provides an identity layer on OAuth 2.0, enabling clients to verify the identity of the end-user based on the authentication performed by an authorization server.

3. Multi-Factor Authentication (MFA): Requires users to provide two or more verification factors to gain access (e.g., password, fingerprint, SMS code), adding an extra layer of security.

Authentication mechanisms play a crucial role in securing web applications and protecting user data. In this guide, we've explored Basic Authentication, Token-Based Authentication using JWT in Flask, and briefly mentioned other mechanisms like OAuth, OpenID Connect, and Multi-Factor Authentication. Choosing the right authentication method depends on factors such as security requirements, user experience, and the nature of the application.

Implementing Authentication with Flask Extensions

Flask is a lightweight and flexible web framework for Python, widely used for building web applications, including APIs. Authentication is a critical aspect of web development, ensuring that only authorized users can access protected resources. In this guide, we'll explore how to implement authentication in Flask using extensions, which provide ready-to-use solutions for various authentication mechanisms.

Flask Extensions for Authentication:

Several Flask extensions simplify the implementation of authentication in Flask applications. These extensions offer features like user management, session handling, and integration with popular authentication protocols. Let's delve into some of the most commonly used Flask extensions for authentication:

1. Flask-Login:

Flask-Login provides user session management for Flask applications, handling the login process, user sessions, and user authentication. It's easy to integrate and can be customized to suit different authentication requirements.

Let's see how to implement authentication with Flask-Login:

```python
from flask import Flask, render_template, request, redirect, url_for
from flask_login import LoginManager, UserMixin, login_user, logout_user, login_required

app = Flask(__name__)
app.config['SECRET_KEY'] = 'your_secret_key'

# Mock user database (for demonstration purposes)
class User(UserMixin):
    def __init__(self, id):
        self.id = id

users = {'user1': {'password': 'password1'}, 'user2': {'password': 'password2'}}
login_manager = LoginManager()
login_manager.init_app(app)

@login_manager.user_loader
def load_user(user_id):
    return User(user_id)
```

```python
@app.route('/login', methods=['GET', 'POST'])
def login():
    if request.method == 'POST':
        username = request.form['username']
        password = request.form['password']
        if username in users and users[username]['password'] == password:
            user = User(username)
            login_user(user)
            return redirect(url_for('protected'))
    return render_template('login.html')

@app.route('/protected')
@login_required
def protected():
    return 'Protected Route'

@app.route('/logout')
def logout():
    logout_user()
    return redirect(url_for('login'))

if __name__ == '__main__':
    app.run(debug=True)
```
```
```

In this implementation, Flask-Login manages user sessions and authentication. The `login_user()` function is used to log in a user, while the `login_required` decorator ensures that only authenticated users can access protected routes.

2. Flask-Security:

Flask-Security is a comprehensive security extension for Flask applications, providing features like user authentication, role-based access control, password hashing, and token authentication.

Let's implement authentication with Flask-Security:

```python
from flask import Flask, render_template, redirect, url_for
from flask_security import Security, login_required, SQLAlchemyUserDatastore, UserMixin, RoleMixin

app = Flask(__name__)
app.config['SECRET_KEY'] = 'your_secret_key'
app.config['SQLALCHEMY_DATABASE_URI'] = 'sqlite:///mydatabase.db'

from flask_sqlalchemy import SQLAlchemy
db = SQLAlchemy(app)
```

```python
# Define User and Role models
roles_users = db.Table('roles_users',
            db.Column('user_id', db.Integer(), db.ForeignKey('user.id')),
            db.Column('role_id', db.Integer(), db.ForeignKey('role.id')))

class Role(db.Model, RoleMixin):
    id = db.Column(db.Integer(), primary_key=True)
    name = db.Column(db.String(80), unique=True)

class User(db.Model, UserMixin):
    id = db.Column(db.Integer, primary_key=True)
    username = db.Column(db.String(255), unique=True)
    password = db.Column(db.String(255))

    roles = db.relationship('Role', secondary=roles_users,
                backref=db.backref('users', lazy='dynamic'))

# Create the database tables
db.create_all()

user_datastore = SQLAlchemyUserDatastore(db, User, Role)
security = Security(app, user_datastore)
```

```
@app.route('/')
def home():
    return render_template('home.html')

@app.route('/protected')
@login_required
def protected():
    return 'Protected Route'

if __name__ == '__main__':
    app.run(debug=True)
```

In this implementation, Flask-Security handles user authentication and role-based access control. Users and roles are defined as SQLAlchemy models, and Flask-Security takes care of user management, password hashing, and access control.

Flask extensions provide convenient solutions for implementing authentication in Flask applications. Whether you prefer the simplicity of Flask-Login or the comprehensive features of Flask-Security, these extensions streamline the authentication process and help secure your web applications effectively. Choose the extension that best fits your project requirements and start building secure and robust Flask applications today!

Session Management: Keeping Users Logged In

Session management is a crucial aspect of web development, especially when it comes to keeping users logged in securely. In this guide, we'll explore how to implement session management in a Python API using Flask, a popular web framework.

What is Session Management?

Session management involves keeping track of user sessions to maintain their state across multiple requests. It allows users to remain authenticated and provides a seamless browsing experience by storing temporary data related to the user's interaction with the application.

Setting Up Flask

First, let's set up a basic Flask application.

```python
from flask import Flask

app = Flask(__name__)

@app.route('/')
def index():
```

```
    return 'Hello, World!'

if __name__ == '__main__':
    app.run(debug=True)
```

Flask Session Management

Flask provides built-in support for session management through the `session` object. We can use this object to store user-specific data securely.

```python
from flask import Flask, session, redirect, url_for, escape, request

app = Flask(__name__)
app.secret_key = b'_5#y2L"F4Q8z\n\xec]/'

@app.route('/')
def index():
    if 'username' in session:
        return 'Logged in as %s' % escape(session['username'])
    return 'You are not logged in'

@app.route('/login', methods=['GET', 'POST'])
def login():
```

```python
    if request.method == 'POST':
        session['username'] = request.form['username']
        return redirect(url_for('index'))
    return '''
        <form method="post">
            <p><input type="text" name="username">
            <p><input type="submit" value="Login">
        </form>
    '''

@app.route('/logout')
def logout():
    session.pop('username', None)
    return redirect(url_for('index'))

if __name__ == '__main__':
    app.run(debug=True)
```

Explanation

- We import the necessary modules from Flask.

- We set a secret key for our application. This is used to cryptographically sign the session cookie.

- The `/login` route handles both GET and POST requests. When the user submits the login form, their username is stored in the session.

- The `/logout` route removes the username from the session, effectively logging the user out.

- The `/` route checks if the user is logged in and displays a message accordingly.

Secure Session Management

It's essential to ensure that session data is stored securely. Flask sessions are secure by default, as long as the `secret_key` is kept secret. Additionally, you can configure the session to use server-side storage rather than client-side cookies for added security.

```python
app.config['SESSION_TYPE'] = 'filesystem'
```

This configuration stores session data on the server's file system instead of the client's cookie. However, this may not be suitable for large-scale applications due to performance considerations.

Session Timeout

To improve security, it's a good practice to implement session timeout. This prevents inactive sessions from being hijacked by unauthorized users.

```python
from datetime import timedelta

app.config['PERMANENT_SESSION_LIFETIME'] = timedelta(minutes=30)
```

This configuration sets the session timeout to 30 minutes. Adjust the value according to your application's requirements.

Session management is essential for maintaining user state and keeping users logged in securely. With Flask, implementing session management is straightforward, thanks to its built-in support for sessions. By following best practices such as setting a secret key, using server-side storage, and implementing session timeout, you can ensure that your application remains secure and provides a seamless user experience.

Chapter 6

Role-Based Access Control (RBAC): Granular Control Over User Permissions

Role-Based Access Control (RBAC) is a powerful method for managing user permissions within an application. With RBAC, access permissions are assigned to roles, and users are assigned one or more roles. This approach provides granular control over who can access what functionality within the application. In this guide, we'll explore how to implement RBAC in a Python API using Flask.

Understanding RBAC

RBAC is based on the principle of least privilege, which means that users are granted only the permissions they need to perform their tasks. This minimizes the risk of unauthorized access to sensitive data and functionality.

In RBAC, there are typically three main entities:

1. Users: Individuals who interact with the application.

2. Roles: Sets of permissions that define what actions users can perform.

3. Permissions: Granular actions or operations that can be performed within the application.

Setting Up Flask

Let's start by setting up a basic Flask application.

```python
from flask import Flask

app = Flask(__name__)

@app.route('/')
def index():
    return 'Hello, World!'

if __name__ == '__main__':
    app.run(debug=True)
```

Implementing RBAC

To implement RBAC in Flask, we can use a combination of decorators, middleware, and role-checking functions.

```python
from functools import wraps
from flask import request, jsonify
```

```python
# Dummy user data
users = {
    'user1': {'username': 'user1', 'password': 'password1', 'roles': ['admin']},
    'user2': {'username': 'user2', 'password': 'password2', 'roles': ['user']}
}

# Dummy permission data
permissions = {
    'admin': ['read', 'write', 'delete'],
    'user': ['read']
}

def authenticate(username, password):
    user = users.get(username)
    if user and user['password'] == password:
        return user

def authorize(role, permission):
    return permission in permissions.get(role, [])

def login_required(f):
    @wraps(f)
    def decorated_function(*args, **kwargs):
        auth = request.authorization
```

```
    if not auth or not authenticate(auth.username,
auth.password):
        return jsonify({'message': 'Authentication
required'}), 401
    return f(*args, **kwargs)
  return decorated_function

def role_required(role):
  def decorator(f):
    @wraps(f)
    def decorated_function(*args, **kwargs):
      auth = request.authorization
      user = authenticate(auth.username,
auth.password)
      if not user:
        return jsonify({'message': 'User not found'}),
404
      if role not in user['roles']:
        return jsonify({'message': 'Insufficient
permissions'}), 403
      return f(*args, **kwargs)
    return decorated_function
  return decorator
```

Usage

Now, let's see how to use these decorators to enforce RBAC in our Flask routes.

```python
@app.route('/admin')
@login_required
@role_required('admin')
def admin_panel():
    return jsonify({'message': 'Welcome to the admin panel!'})

@app.route('/user')
@login_required
@role_required('user')
def user_dashboard():
    return jsonify({'message': 'Welcome to your dashboard!'})
```

In the above example:

- The `@login_required` decorator ensures that the user is authenticated before accessing the route.

- The `@role_required` decorator checks if the authenticated user has the specified role before allowing access to the route.

Role-Based Access Control (RBAC) is a powerful mechanism for managing user permissions within an application. By assigning roles to users and defining permissions for each role, you can enforce granular access control and ensure that users only have access to the functionality they need. In Flask, implementing RBAC can be achieved using decorators and middleware to authenticate users and check their roles before allowing access to certain routes. By following RBAC best practices, you can enhance the security of your application and protect sensitive data from unauthorized access.

Protecting Specific Resources and Endpoints

Protecting specific resources and endpoints is crucial for ensuring the security of your API. By restricting access to certain routes or resources, you can prevent unauthorized users from accessing sensitive data or functionality. In this guide, we'll explore various techniques for protecting specific resources and endpoints in a Python API built with Flask.

Understanding Endpoint Protection

Endpoint protection involves implementing mechanisms to control access to specific routes or resources within your API. This can be achieved through authentication, authorization, rate limiting, and other security measures.

Setting Up Flask

Let's start by setting up a basic Flask application.

```python
from flask import Flask

app = Flask(__name__)

@app.route('/')
def index():
    return 'Hello, World!'

if __name__ == '__main__':
    app.run(debug=True)
```

Implementing Endpoint Protection

Authentication

Authentication is the process of verifying the identity of users accessing your API. This can be done using various methods such as token-based authentication, OAuth, or basic authentication.

```python
```

```python
from flask import request, jsonify

@app.route('/protected')
def protected_resource():
    auth = request.authorization
    if not auth or not authenticate(auth.username, auth.password):
        return jsonify({'message': 'Authentication required'}), 401
    return jsonify({'message': 'Access granted'})
```

Authorization

Authorization determines whether authenticated users have permission to access specific resources or endpoints within your API. This can be based on roles, permissions, or other criteria.

```python
@app.route('/admin')
def admin_panel():
    if not user_has_permission('admin'):
        return jsonify({'message': 'Unauthorized'}), 403
    return jsonify({'message': 'Welcome to the admin panel!'})
```

Rate Limiting

Rate limiting restricts the number of requests that users can make to specific endpoints within a given time period. This helps prevent abuse or DoS attacks.

```python
from flask_limiter import Limiter
from flask_limiter.util import get_remote_address

limiter = Limiter(
    app,
    key_func=get_remote_address,
    default_limits=["100 per day", "10 per hour"]
)

@app.route('/limited')
@limiter.limit("10 per minute")
def limited_resource():
    return jsonify({'message': 'Access granted'})
```

Protecting specific resources and endpoints is essential for ensuring the security and integrity of your API. By implementing authentication, authorization, rate limiting, and other security measures, you can control access to sensitive data and functionality, prevent abuse, and safeguard your API against various threats. In Flask, you can use built-in features and extensions to easily implement endpoint protection and enhance the security of your application. By following best practices and staying informed about emerging security threats, you can create a robust and secure API that meets the needs of your users and stakeholders.

Best Practices for Secure Authorization

Securing authorization is crucial for protecting your application's resources and ensuring that only authorized users have access to sensitive data and functionality. In this guide, we'll explore best practices for secure authorization in a Python API developed with Flask.

1. Principle of Least Privilege

The principle of least privilege states that users should only be given the minimum level of access necessary to perform their tasks. This minimizes the potential impact of a security breach. When implementing authorization, carefully define roles and permissions to ensure that users have access only to the resources and functionality they need.

2. Centralized Authorization Logic

Centralize your authorization logic to ensure consistency and maintainability. Avoid scattering authorization checks throughout your codebase. Instead, implement a centralized mechanism for enforcing access control, such as decorators or middleware, that can be easily applied to endpoints or resources.

3. Role-Based Access Control (RBAC)

RBAC is a popular authorization model that assigns roles to users and grants permissions to those roles. Implement RBAC in your Flask application by defining roles and mapping them to specific permissions. Use decorators or middleware to enforce role-based access control on endpoints.

```python
from functools import wraps
from flask import request, jsonify

def role_required(role):
    def decorator(f):
        @wraps(f)
        def decorated_function(*args, **kwargs):
            # Check if user has the required role
            if not user_has_role(role):
                return jsonify({'message': 'Insufficient permissions'}), 403
            return f(*args, **kwargs)
        return decorated_function
```

```
    return decorator
```

```
@app.route('/admin')
@role_required('admin')
def admin_panel():
    return jsonify({'message': 'Welcome to the admin panel!'})
```

4. Secure Storage of Credentials

Ensure that user credentials, such as passwords or API keys, are stored securely. Use strong encryption and hashing algorithms to protect sensitive information. Avoid storing plaintext passwords and use secure hashing techniques like bcrypt or PBKDF2.

5. Token-Based Authentication

Implement token-based authentication for API endpoints. When a user logs in successfully, issue a JSON Web Token (JWT) containing user information and permissions. Require clients to include this token in subsequent requests to access protected resources. Verify and decode the token on the server to authenticate users and enforce access control.

```python
```

```python
import jwt

@app.route('/login', methods=['POST'])
def login():
    # Validate user credentials
    # Generate JWT token
    token = jwt.encode({'username': 'user1', 'roles': ['admin']}, app.config['SECRET_KEY'])
    return jsonify({'token': token})

@app.route('/protected')
def protected_resource():
    token = request.headers.get('Authorization')
    if not token:
        return jsonify({'message': 'Authorization required'}), 401
    try:
        payload = jwt.decode(token, app.config['SECRET_KEY'], algorithms=['HS256'])
        # Check user permissions
        if 'admin' not in payload['roles']:
            return jsonify({'message': 'Insufficient permissions'}), 403
        return jsonify({'message': 'Access granted'})
    except jwt.ExpiredSignatureError:
        return jsonify({'message': 'Token expired'}), 401
    except jwt.InvalidTokenError:
        return jsonify({'message': 'Invalid token'}), 401
```

```

## 6. Secure Communication with HTTPS

Ensure that communication between clients and your API server is encrypted using HTTPS. This prevents eavesdropping and man-in-the-middle attacks, protecting sensitive data and credentials exchanged between the client and server.

## 7. Logging and Monitoring

Implement logging and monitoring to track authentication and authorization events, detect suspicious activity, and troubleshoot issues. Log access attempts, authentication failures, and authorization errors to a secure and centralized location for analysis and auditing.

Securing authorization in your Flask API is essential for protecting your application's resources and data from unauthorized access and malicious attacks. By following best practices such as implementing RBAC, token-based authentication, secure credential storage, and HTTPS communication, you can create a robust and secure authorization mechanism that meets the needs of your application and users. Additionally, regularly review and update your authorization logic to adapt to evolving
```

security threats and maintain the integrity of your application's security posture.

Chapter 7

Unit Testing: Isolating and Validating Individual Components

Unit testing is a fundamental practice in software development that involves testing individual components of your application in isolation to ensure they function correctly. In the context of a Python API developed with Flask, unit testing allows you to verify the behavior of endpoints, functions, and modules, helping to catch bugs early and maintain the stability of your codebase. In this guide, we'll explore how to implement unit testing for a Flask API and best practices for writing effective tests.

Setting Up Flask for Testing

Before writing unit tests, let's set up a basic Flask application and configure it for testing.

```python
from flask import Flask

app = Flask(__name__)

@app.route('/')
def index():
    return 'Hello, World!'
```

```
if __name__ == '__main__':
    app.run(debug=True)
```

Writing Unit Tests with pytest

We'll use pytest, a popular testing framework for Python, to write and run our unit tests. First, install pytest using pip:

```bash
pip install pytest
```

Now, let's create a test file named `test_app.py` to write our unit tests.

```python
import pytest
from app import app

@pytest.fixture
def client():
    with app.test_client() as client:
        yield client

def test_index(client):
```

```
response = client.get('/')
assert response.status_code == 200
assert b'Hello, World!' in response.data
```

In this test file:

- We use the `pytest.fixture` decorator to define a fixture named `client`, which creates a test client for our Flask application.

- The `test_index` function uses this fixture to send a GET request to the root endpoint (`/`) and asserts that the response status code is 200 (OK) and that the response data contains the expected message.

Running Unit Tests

To run our unit tests, simply execute the pytest command in the terminal:

```bash
pytest
```

pytest will discover and run all test functions in files named `test_*.py` in the current directory and its subdirectories.

Best Practices for Unit Testing

1. Test One Thing at a Time

Write focused tests that verify the behavior of individual components or functions. Avoid testing multiple functionalities in a single test, as this can make it harder to pinpoint the cause of failures.

2. Use Descriptive Test Names

Use descriptive names for your test functions that clearly indicate what aspect of the code they are testing. This makes it easier to understand the purpose of each test and identify failing tests quickly.

3. Use Fixtures for Setup and Teardown

Use pytest fixtures to set up preconditions for your tests, such as creating test data or initializing resources. This helps keep your test code clean and avoids duplication of setup code across multiple tests.

4. Mock External Dependencies

Use mocking to simulate the behavior of external dependencies, such as databases or external APIs, during testing. This allows you to isolate the component being tested and focus on its behavior without relying on the behavior of external systems.

```python
from unittest.mock import MagicMock

def test_function_with_mock():
    mock_dependency = MagicMock()
    mock_dependency.some_method.return_value = 'mocked response'

    result = function_under_test(mock_dependency)

    assert result == 'mocked response'
    mock_dependency.some_method.assert_called_once()
```

5. Test Edge Cases and Error Conditions

Ensure your tests cover edge cases and error conditions to verify that your code behaves correctly under different scenarios. Test input validation, error handling, and boundary conditions to catch potential bugs and improve the robustness of your code.

Unit testing is an essential practice for ensuring the reliability and maintainability of your Flask API. By writing focused, descriptive tests that verify the behavior of individual components in isolation, you can catch bugs early, prevent regressions, and build confidence in your codebase. Follow best practices such as using fixtures for setup and teardown, mocking external dependencies, and testing edge cases to create comprehensive test suites that provide thorough coverage of your API's functionality. By investing in unit testing, you can improve the quality of your code and deliver more reliable software to your users.

Integration Testing: Ensuring Different Parts of Your API Work Together Seamlessly

Integration testing is an essential part of software development that focuses on testing the interactions between different components of your application to ensure they work together seamlessly. In the context of a Python API developed with Flask, integration testing involves testing the integration of endpoints, modules, databases, and external services to verify that the API functions correctly as a whole. In this guide, we'll explore how to implement integration testing for a Flask API and best practices for writing effective tests.

Setting Up Flask for Integration Testing

Before writing integration tests, let's set up a Flask application and configure it for testing. We'll also set up a database for our API to interact with.

```python
from flask import Flask
from flask_sqlalchemy import SQLAlchemy

app = Flask(__name__)
app.config['SQLALCHEMY_DATABASE_URI'] = 'sqlite:///test.db'
db = SQLAlchemy(app)

class User(db.Model):
    id = db.Column(db.Integer, primary_key=True)
    username = db.Column(db.String(80), unique=True, nullable=False)

    def __repr__(self):
        return '<User %r>' % self.username

@app.route('/')
def index():
    return 'Hello, World!'

if __name__ == '__main__':
    app.run(debug=True)
```

```

## **Writing Integration Tests with pytest**

We'll use pytest to write and run our integration tests. First, install pytest and Flask testing extensions using pip:

```bash
pip install pytest flask-testing
```

Now, let's create a test file named `test_integration.py` to write our integration tests.

```python
import pytest
from app import app, db, User

@pytest.fixture
def client():
    app.config['TESTING'] = True
    with app.test_client() as client:
        yield client

@pytest.fixture
def database():
    db.create_all()
```
```

```
    user1 = User(username='testuser1')
    user2 = User(username='testuser2')
    db.session.add(user1)
    db.session.add(user2)
    db.session.commit()
    yield db
    db.drop_all()

def test_index(client):
    response = client.get('/')
    assert response.status_code == 200
    assert b'Hello, World!' in response.data

def test_get_users(client, database):
    response = client.get('/users')
    assert response.status_code == 200
    assert b'testuser1' in response.data
    assert b'testuser2' in response.data
```

In this test file:

- We use fixtures to set up a test client (`client`) for our Flask application and initialize a test database (`database`) for interacting with our models.

- The `test_index` function sends a GET request to the root endpoint (`/`) and asserts that the response status code is 200 (OK) and that the response data contains the expected message.

- The `test_get_users` function sends a GET request to an endpoint (`/users`) that retrieves user data from the database. It asserts that the response status code is 200 and that the response data contains the expected user information.

Running Integration Tests

To run our integration tests, simply execute the pytest command in the terminal:

```bash
pytest
```

pytest will discover and run all test functions in files named `test_*.py` in the current directory and its subdirectories.

Best Practices for Integration Testing

1. Use Realistic Test Data

Use realistic test data in your integration tests to simulate real-world scenarios and ensure that your API behaves correctly under typical conditions. Populate your test database with sample data that represents different use cases and edge cases.

2. Test Endpoints with Various Input Parameters

Test your API endpoints with various input parameters, payloads, and HTTP methods to verify that they handle different types of requests correctly. Include test cases for both valid and invalid input to ensure robust input validation and error handling.

3. Test Database Interactions

Test the interaction between your API and the database to ensure that data is stored, retrieved, and updated correctly. Use fixtures to set up and tear down test databases for each test run, and verify the integrity of the data using assertions.

4. Mock External Services

Mock external services, such as third-party APIs or microservices, during integration testing to isolate your API from external dependencies and ensure reliable test results. Use mocking libraries or test doubles to simulate the behavior of external services and control their responses.

5. Test Error Handling and Edge Cases

Test error handling and edge cases in your integration tests to verify that your API behaves gracefully in unexpected situations. Include test cases for scenarios such as network failures, database errors, and unexpected input to ensure that your API provides informative error messages and handles exceptions correctly.

Integration testing is an essential practice for ensuring the reliability and functionality of your Flask API. By writing comprehensive integration tests that verify the interaction between different components of your application, you can catch bugs early, detect integration issues, and ensure that your API works as expected in a production environment. Follow best practices such as using realistic test data, testing endpoints with various input parameters, and verifying database interactions to create robust integration test suites that provide thorough coverage of your API's functionality. By investing in integration testing, you can build confidence in your codebase and deliver a high-quality API to your users.

Test-Driven Development (TDD): A Proactive Approach to Building Robust APIs

Test-Driven Development (TDD) is a software development methodology that emphasizes writing tests before writing code. It follows a cycle of writing a failing test, writing the code to pass the test, and then refactoring the code to improve its design. TDD helps developers create robust and reliable APIs by ensuring that each component is thoroughly tested and meets the requirements specified by the tests. In this guide, we'll explore how to implement TDD in a Python API developed with Flask.

Understanding Test-Driven Development

TDD consists of the following steps:

1. Write a Test: Start by writing a test that defines the desired behavior or functionality of the API component you're working on. This test should fail initially because the corresponding code hasn't been implemented yet.

2. Write Code to Pass the Test: Write the minimum amount of code necessary to make the test pass. This code should fulfill the requirements specified by the test, but it doesn't need to be perfect or complete.

3. Run the Test: Run the test to verify that it passes. If the test fails, refine the code until the test passes.

4. Refactor the Code: Once the test passes, refactor the code to improve its design, readability, and performance. Ensure that the test still passes after refactoring.

5. Repeat: Repeat the cycle for each new feature or functionality, writing tests to define the desired behavior and implementing the corresponding code to fulfill those requirements.

Setting Up Flask for TDD

Before we begin implementing TDD for our Flask API, let's set up a basic Flask application and configure it for testing.

```python
from flask import Flask

app = Flask(__name__)

@app.route('/')
def index():
    return 'Hello, World!'

if __name__ == '__main__':
```

```
app.run(debug=True)
```

Writing Tests with pytest

We'll use pytest to write our tests. First, install pytest using pip:

```bash
pip install pytest
```

Now, let's create a test file named `test_tdd.py` to write our tests.

```python
import pytest
from app import app

@pytest.fixture
def client():
    app.config['TESTING'] = True
    with app.test_client() as client:
        yield client

def test_index(client):
    response = client.get('/')
    assert response.status_code == 200
```

```
assert b'Hello, World!' in response.data
```

In this test file:

- We use a pytest fixture to set up a test client (`client`) for our Flask application with testing mode enabled.

- The `test_index` function sends a GET request to the root endpoint (`/`) and asserts that the response status code is 200 (OK) and that the response data contains the expected message.

Implementing TDD for Flask APIs

Now that we have our testing infrastructure in place, let's implement TDD for a simple API endpoint that returns a JSON response.

Step 1: Write a Failing Test

Start by writing a test that defines the behavior of the API endpoint you want to implement. For example, let's write a test for an endpoint that returns a JSON response with a specific message.

```python
```

```
def test_hello_json(client):
    response = client.get('/hello')
    assert response.status_code == 200
    assert response.json == {'message': 'Hello, JSON!'}
```

Step 2: Write Code to Pass the Test

Now, write the code necessary to make the test pass. Implement the `/hello` endpoint in your Flask application to return a JSON response with the specified message.

```python
from flask import jsonify

@app.route('/hello')
def hello():
    return jsonify({'message': 'Hello, JSON!'})
```

Step 3: Run the Test

Run the test to verify that it passes. If the test fails, refine the code until the test passes.

```bash
pytest
```

```

## Step 4: Refactor the Code

Once the test passes, refactor the code to improve its design, readability, and performance. Ensure that the test still passes after refactoring.

```python
from flask import jsonify

@app.route('/hello')
def hello():
    return jsonify(message='Hello, JSON!')
```

Best Practices for Test-Driven Development

1. Write Small, Focused Tests

Write small, focused tests that test one specific behavior or functionality at a time. This makes it easier to pinpoint the cause of failures and maintain the test suite over time.

2. Use Descriptive Test Names
```

Use descriptive names for your test functions that clearly indicate what aspect of the code they are testing. This makes it easier to understand the purpose of each test and identify failing tests quickly.

3. Write Tests First

Follow the TDD cycle by writing tests before writing code. This helps clarify the requirements and expectations for each component before implementation begins.

4. Refactor Regularly

Refactor your code regularly to improve its design, readability, and performance. Ensure that the test suite provides adequate coverage and that all tests still pass after refactoring.

5. Aim for 100% Code Coverage

Strive for 100% code coverage by writing tests for all code paths and edge cases. While achieving 100% code coverage doesn't guarantee bug-free code, it helps identify areas of your codebase that may need additional testing or attention.

Test-Driven Development (TDD) is a proactive approach to building robust APIs that emphasizes writing tests before writing code. By following the TDD cycle of writing failing tests, writing code to pass the tests, and refactoring the code, developers can create APIs that are thoroughly tested and meet the requirements specified by the tests. In Flask, TDD can be implemented using pytest and fixtures to write tests that define the desired behavior of each API component and verify that the implementation fulfills those requirements. By embracing TDD, developers can improve the reliability, maintainability, and quality of their Flask APIs while reducing the risk of introducing bugs and regressions.

Popular Testing Frameworks for Flask: Unittest, pytest, and More

When it comes to testing Flask applications, there are several popular testing frameworks available, each with its own set of features and capabilities. In this guide, we'll explore two of the most commonly used testing frameworks for Flask: unittest and pytest. We'll discuss their features, syntax, and best practices for writing tests in Flask applications.

unittest

unittest is the built-in testing framework in Python, inspired by the JUnit testing framework for Java. It provides a comprehensive set of tools for writing and running tests, including test discovery, test fixtures, and test runners.

Writing Tests with unittest

Let's start by writing a simple test using unittest for a Flask application.

```python
import unittest
from app import app

class TestApp(unittest.TestCase):
    def setUp(self):
        self.app = app.test_client()

    def test_index(self):
        response = self.app.get('/')
        self.assertEqual(response.status_code, 200)
        self.assertIn(b'Hello, World!', response.data)

if __name__ == '__main__':
    unittest.main()
```

In this example:

- We create a subclass of `unittest.TestCase` named `TestApp` to define our test cases.

- We use the `setUp` method to set up a test client (`self.app`) for our Flask application before each test case.

- We define a test method named `test_index` that sends a GET request to the root endpoint (`/`) and asserts that the response status code is 200 (OK) and that the response data contains the expected message.

Running Tests with unittest

To run our unittest tests, simply execute the test file in the terminal:

```bash
python test_unittest.py
```

pytest

pytest is a popular testing framework for Python that provides a more concise and flexible syntax for writing tests compared to unittest. It offers powerful features such as test parametrization, fixtures, and plugins, making it a versatile choice for testing Flask applications.

Writing Tests with pytest

Let's rewrite the previous test using pytest to see how it compares to unittest.

```python
import pytest
from app import app

@pytest.fixture
def client():
    app.config['TESTING'] = True
    with app.test_client() as client:
        yield client

def test_index(client):
    response = client.get('/')
    assert response.status_code == 200
    assert b'Hello, World!' in response.data
```

In this pytest example:

- We use a pytest fixture named `client` to set up a test client for our Flask application with testing mode enabled.

- We define a test function named `test_index` that sends a GET request to the root endpoint (`/`) and uses pytest's assertion syntax to check the response status code and content.

Running Tests with pytest

To run our pytest tests, simply execute the pytest command in the terminal:

```bash
pytest
```

Choosing Between unittest and pytest

Both unittest and pytest have their strengths and weaknesses, and the choice between them ultimately depends on your preferences and requirements.

unittest

- **Built-in:** unittest comes with the Python standard library, so you don't need to install any additional dependencies to use it.

- **Comprehensive**: unittest provides a comprehensive set of tools for writing and running tests, including test discovery, test fixtures, and test runners.

- **Familiar Syntax:** If you're familiar with JUnit or other xUnit-style testing frameworks, you'll find unittest's syntax familiar and easy to understand.

pytest

- **Concise Syntax:** pytest's syntax is more concise and expressive compared to unittest, making it easier to write and read tests.

- **Powerful Features:** pytest offers powerful features such as test parametrization, fixtures, and plugins, allowing you to write complex tests with less boilerplate code.

- **Flexible**: pytest is more flexible and extensible than unittest, allowing you to customize and extend its behavior using plugins and custom fixtures.

Best Practices for Testing Flask Applications

Regardless of the testing framework you choose, here are some best practices for testing Flask applications:

1. Isolate Tests: Keep tests independent and isolated from each other to ensure that failures in one test don't affect the execution of other tests.

2. Use Fixtures: Use fixtures to set up preconditions for your tests, such as creating test data or initializing resources. This helps keep your test code clean and avoids duplication of setup code across multiple tests.

3. Test Edge Cases: Test edge cases and error conditions to verify that your Flask application behaves correctly under different scenarios. Include test cases for both valid and invalid input to ensure robust input validation and error handling.

4. Mock External Dependencies: Mock external dependencies, such as databases or external APIs, during testing to isolate your Flask application from external dependencies and ensure reliable test results.

5. Use Continuous Integration: Set up continuous integration (CI) to automatically run your tests whenever changes are made to your Flask application's codebase. This helps catch bugs early and ensures that your application remains reliable and stable.

unittest and pytest are two popular testing frameworks for Flask applications, each with its own set of features and capabilities. Both frameworks allow you to write and run tests for your Flask application, helping you ensure that your code behaves as expected and remains reliable and robust. Whether you prefer the familiarity of unittest or the flexibility of pytest, adopting a testing framework is essential for building and maintaining high-quality Flask applications. By following best practices for testing Flask applications and choosing the right testing framework for your needs, you can create reliable, bug-free applications that meet the requirements of your users.

Chapter 8

Setting Up a Local Development Server for Testing and Iteration

Setting up a local development server for testing and iteration is crucial for efficiently developing and debugging Flask APIs. In this guide, we'll walk through the steps to set up a local development server for testing and iteration, including configuring Flask, installing dependencies, and running the server. We'll also cover best practices for local development to ensure a smooth and productive development experience.

Setting Up Flask

Before setting up the local development server, let's create a basic Flask application to work with.

```python
from flask import Flask

app = Flask(__name__)

@app.route('/')
def index():
    return 'Hello, World!'
```

```
if __name__ == '__main__':
    app.run(debug=True)
```

Installing Dependencies

To set up a local development server for testing and iteration, you'll need to install Flask and any other dependencies required for your Flask application. You can use pip, the Python package manager, to install Flask and other dependencies.

```bash
pip install flask
```

Configuring Flask for Local Development

Flask provides built-in support for local development through the `app.run()` method. By passing the `debug=True` argument to `app.run()`, Flask will automatically reload the server when code changes are detected and provide detailed error messages in the browser.

```python
if __name__ == '__main__':
    app.run(debug=True)
```

```

## Running the Local Development Server

With Flask configured for local development, you can now run the local development server by executing the Flask application script in your terminal.

```bash
python app.py
```

This command will start the Flask development server on your local machine, allowing you to access your Flask application in a web browser at `http://localhost:5000`.

Best Practices for Local Development

1. Use a Virtual Environment

To avoid conflicts between dependencies and ensure a clean development environment, it's recommended to use a virtual environment for your Flask project. You can create a virtual environment using the `venv` module, which is included with Python.

```bash

```
python -m venv venv
```

Activate the virtual environment:

- On Windows:

```bash
venv\Scripts\activate
```

- On macOS and Linux:

```bash
source venv/bin/activate
```

2. Separate Configuration for Development

Use separate configuration settings for development, testing, and production environments. Flask allows you to define different configuration settings for each environment, making it easy to customize behavior based on the deployment environment.

```python
app.config['DEBUG'] = True
```

3. Logging and Debugging

Use logging and debugging tools to troubleshoot issues and track the execution of your Flask application during development. Flask provides built-in support for logging, and you can enable additional debugging features to get detailed information about request handling, routing, and template rendering.

```python
app.logger.setLevel(logging.DEBUG)
```

4. Interactive Debugging with Flask Debugger

Flask provides a built-in debugger called the Flask Debugger, which provides an interactive interface for debugging your Flask application in real-time. You can enable the Flask Debugger by setting the `debug` parameter to `True` in `app.run()`.

```python
if __name__ == '__main__':
    app.run(debug=True)
```

5. Version Control with Git

Use version control with Git to track changes to your Flask application's codebase and collaborate with other developers. Version control allows you to revert changes, track issues, and manage project milestones effectively.

```bash
git init
git add .
git commit -m "Initial commit"
```

6. Code Quality and Style

Maintain code quality and style by following Python's PEP 8 style guide and using tools like flake8 and pylint to enforce coding standards and identify potential issues in your codebase.

```bash
pip install flake8 pylint
```

Setting up a local development server for testing and iteration is essential for efficiently developing and debugging Flask APIs. By following the steps outlined in this guide and adhering to best practices for local development, you can create a productive development environment that facilitates rapid iteration, troubleshooting, and collaboration. With Flask's built-in support for local development, along with tools like virtual environments, logging, debugging, and version control, you can streamline the development process and deliver high-quality Flask applications that meet the needs of your users.

Deployment Options: Cloud Platforms like Heroku and AWS

Deploying a Flask API to cloud platforms like Heroku and AWS (Amazon Web Services) provides scalable, reliable, and cost-effective options for hosting your application. In this guide, we'll explore how to deploy a Flask API to Heroku and AWS, including configuring the deployment environment, setting up the necessary services, and deploying the application. We'll also cover best practices for deployment to ensure a smooth and successful deployment process.

Deploying to Heroku

Heroku is a popular platform-as-a-service (PaaS) that allows you to deploy, manage, and scale web applications with ease. Follow these steps to deploy a Flask API to Heroku:

1. Install Heroku CLI

First, install the Heroku Command Line Interface (CLI) to interact with Heroku from your terminal.

```bash
brew tap heroku/brew && brew install heroku
```

2. Initialize Git Repository

If your Flask application isn't already under version control with Git, initialize a Git repository in your project directory.

```bash
git init
```

3. Create a Heroku App

Create a new Heroku app using the Heroku CLI. Replace `my-flask-app` with your desired app name.

```bash
heroku create my-flask-app
```

4. Configure Procfile

Create a `Procfile` in your project directory to specify the commands Heroku should use to run your Flask application.

```bash
echo "web: gunicorn app:app" > Procfile
```

5. Specify Dependencies

Create a `requirements.txt` file containing the dependencies for your Flask application. You can generate this file using pip.

```bash
pip freeze > requirements.txt
```

6. Deploy to Heroku

Commit your changes and deploy your Flask application to Heroku using Git.

```bash
git add .
git commit -m "Initial deployment to Heroku"
```

```
git push heroku master
```

7. Access Your App

Once the deployment is complete, you can access your Flask API by visiting the URL provided by Heroku.

```bash
heroku open
```

Deploying to AWS (Amazon Web Services)

AWS provides a range of services for deploying and managing web applications, including Elastic Beanstalk, Lambda, and EC2. We'll focus on deploying a Flask API to Elastic Beanstalk, a service that simplifies the deployment, scaling, and management of web applications.

1. Install AWS CLI

Install the AWS Command Line Interface (CLI) to interact with AWS from your terminal.

```bash
pip install awscli
```

```

## 2. Configure AWS CLI

Configure the AWS CLI with your AWS credentials. You can obtain your access key ID and secret access key from the AWS Management Console.

```bash
aws configure
```

3. Initialize Elastic Beanstalk Application

Initialize an Elastic Beanstalk application using the AWS CLI. Replace `my-flask-app` with your desired application name.

```bash
eb init -p python-3.8 my-flask-app
```

4. Create Environment

Create an environment for your Elastic Beanstalk application. You can choose between a web server environment (`WebServer`) and a worker environment
```

(`Worker`) depending on your application's requirements.

```bash
eb create my-flask-env
```

5. Deploy Application

Deploy your Flask application to the Elastic Beanstalk environment.

```bash
eb deploy
```

6. Access Your App

Once the deployment is complete, you can access your Flask API by visiting the URL provided by Elastic Beanstalk.

```bash
eb open
```

Best Practices for Deployment

Regardless of the deployment platform you choose, here are some best practices to ensure a smooth and successful deployment process:

1. Environment Configuration: Use environment variables to store sensitive information such as database credentials and API keys. This helps keep your application secure and portable across different environments.

2. Automated Testing: Set up automated testing using CI/CD (Continuous Integration/Continuous Deployment) tools like Travis CI or CircleCI to ensure that your application passes tests before deploying to production.

3. Monitoring and Logging: Implement monitoring and logging solutions to track the performance, availability, and errors of your deployed application. Services like AWS CloudWatch and Heroku Metrics provide insights into your application's behavior.

4. Scalability: Design your application to be scalable by leveraging cloud services like AWS Elastic Beanstalk, which can automatically scale your application based on demand.

5. Security: Follow security best practices, such as using HTTPS, securing sensitive endpoints with authentication and authorization, and regularly updating dependencies to patch security vulnerabilities.

Deploying a Flask API to cloud platforms like Heroku and AWS provides scalable, reliable, and cost-effective options for hosting your application. By following the steps outlined in this guide and adhering to best practices for deployment, you can ensure a smooth and successful deployment process and deliver a high-quality Flask API to your users. Whether you choose Heroku or AWS for deployment, both platforms offer powerful features and tools to help you deploy, manage, and scale your Flask API with ease. With Heroku, you can quickly deploy your Flask application with minimal configuration, while AWS provides more flexibility and control over your deployment environment.

Whichever platform you choose, remember to test your deployment thoroughly and monitor your application's performance and security post-deployment. By following best practices and leveraging the features provided by Heroku, AWS, or other cloud platforms, you can deploy a robust and reliable Flask API that meets the needs of your users.

Configuration Management for Production Environments

Configuration management for production environments is crucial for deploying and maintaining Flask APIs at scale. In this guide, we'll explore best practices and techniques for managing configurations in production environments, including handling sensitive information, managing environment-specific settings, and ensuring consistency across deployments. We'll also provide code examples and discuss how to implement configuration management effectively in Flask applications.

Configuration Management in Flask

In Flask, configuration management is typically handled using configuration objects. These objects store key-value pairs representing configuration settings for your Flask application. Flask provides a built-in configuration object named `Config`, but you can also define custom configuration objects for different environments (e.g., development, testing, production).

Example of a Flask Configuration Object

```python
class Config:
    DEBUG = False
```

```
    SECRET_KEY = 'my_secret_key'
    DATABASE_URI = 'sqlite:///app.db'

class ProductionConfig(Config):
    DATABASE_URI = 'postgresql://user:password@localhost/db_name'

class DevelopmentConfig(Config):
    DEBUG = True

class TestingConfig(Config):
    TESTING = True
```

Environment Variables

One common approach for managing configurations in production environments is to use environment variables. Environment variables provide a way to pass configuration values to your Flask application without hardcoding them in your codebase. This allows for greater flexibility and security, as sensitive information such as database credentials can be stored securely outside of the codebase.

Example: Using Environment Variables in Flask

```python
```

```
import os

class Config:
    DEBUG = False
    SECRET_KEY = os.environ.get('SECRET_KEY')
    DATABASE_URI = os.environ.get('DATABASE_URI')

# Set environment variables in production server
# export SECRET_KEY='my_secret_key'
# export DATABASE_URI='postgresql://user:password@localhost/db_name'
```

Configuration Files

Another approach for managing configurations in production environments is to use configuration files. Configuration files allow you to specify environment-specific settings and easily switch between different configurations. Flask supports various file formats for configuration files, including `.ini`, `.json`, and `.yaml`.

Example: Using a JSON Configuration File in Flask

```json
{
```

```
  "DEBUG": false,
  "SECRET_KEY": "my_secret_key",
  "DATABASE_URI": "postgresql://user:password@localhost/db_name"
}
```

Best Practices

Here are some best practices for configuration management in production environments:

1. Use Environment Variables for Sensitive Information: Store sensitive information such as database credentials, API keys, and secret keys in environment variables to prevent them from being exposed in your codebase.

2. Separate Configuration for Different Environments: Define separate configuration objects or files for different environments (e.g., development, testing, production) to ensure that each environment has its own settings.

3. Avoid Hardcoding Configuration Values: Avoid hardcoding configuration values directly in your codebase, as this can make it difficult to manage and maintain configurations, especially in large applications.

4. Automate Configuration Deployment: Use automation tools and scripts to deploy and manage configuration changes across different environments, ensuring consistency and reducing the risk of errors.

5. Encrypt Sensitive Information: Encrypt sensitive information such as database credentials and API keys before storing them in configuration files or environment variables to enhance security.

Configuration management is a critical aspect of deploying Flask APIs in production environments. By following best practices and using techniques such as environment variables and configuration files, you can effectively manage configurations, ensure security, and maintain consistency across deployments. Whether you choose to use environment variables, configuration files, or a combination of both, it's essential to implement a robust configuration management strategy to support the scalability and reliability of your Flask applications in production.

Monitoring and Logging: Keeping an Eye on Your Deployed API

Monitoring and logging are essential aspects of maintaining a healthy and reliable Flask API in production environments. By implementing effective monitoring and logging strategies, you can track the performance, availability, and behavior of your deployed API, identify issues proactively, and ensure a smooth user experience. In this guide, we'll explore best practices for monitoring and logging Flask APIs, including how to set up monitoring tools, configure logging, and analyze logs to troubleshoot issues effectively.

Monitoring Tools for Flask APIs

There are various monitoring tools and services available for monitoring Flask APIs in production environments. These tools provide real-time insights into the performance, availability, and health of your API, allowing you to detect and respond to issues quickly. Some popular monitoring tools for Flask APIs include:

1. Prometheus: Prometheus is an open-source monitoring and alerting toolkit designed for monitoring containerized applications. It provides powerful querying capabilities, visualization tools, and alerting features to help you monitor your Flask API effectively.

2. Grafana: Grafana is an open-source analytics and monitoring platform that integrates with Prometheus and other data sources to visualize and analyze metrics and logs. It offers customizable dashboards and visualization options to monitor the performance and health of your Flask API.

3. New Relic: New Relic is a cloud-based application performance monitoring (APM) solution that provides real-time insights into the performance and behavior of your Flask API. It offers features such as application profiling, distributed tracing, and error tracking to help you identify and troubleshoot performance issues quickly.

4. Datadog: Datadog is a cloud-based monitoring and analytics platform that provides comprehensive monitoring for Flask APIs and other applications. It offers features such as infrastructure monitoring, application performance monitoring (APM), and log management to help you monitor and optimize the performance of your Flask API.

Setting Up Monitoring with Prometheus and Grafana

Let's explore how to set up monitoring for a Flask API using Prometheus and Grafana:

1. Install Prometheus

First, install Prometheus on your server or container where your Flask API is deployed. You can download

Prometheus from the official website or use a package manager to install it.

```bash
# Example installation using apt (for Debian-based systems)
sudo apt-get update
sudo apt-get install prometheus
```

2. Configure Prometheus

Configure Prometheus to scrape metrics from your Flask API. You can define scraping targets in the `prometheus.yml` configuration file.

```yaml
global:
  scrape_interval: 15s

scrape_configs:
  - job_name: 'flask-api'
    static_configs:
      - targets: ['localhost:5000']
```

3. Install Grafana

Next, install Grafana on your server or container to visualize and analyze metrics collected by Prometheus.

```bash
# Example installation using apt (for Debian-based systems)
sudo apt-get install grafana
```

4. Configure Grafana

Configure Grafana to connect to Prometheus as a data source. You can do this by adding Prometheus as a data source in the Grafana UI and specifying the URL of your Prometheus server.

5. Create Dashboards

Create custom dashboards in Grafana to visualize metrics collected by Prometheus. You can create dashboards to monitor various aspects of your Flask API, such as request latency, error rate, and resource usage.

Logging in Flask APIs

In addition to monitoring, logging is essential for tracking the behavior of your Flask API and diagnosing issues in production environments. Flask provides built-in support for logging, allowing you to log messages at different severity levels (e.g., INFO, WARNING, ERROR) and customize logging configurations to suit your needs.

Example: Configuring Logging in Flask

```python
import logging
from flask import Flask

app = Flask(__name__)

# Configure logging
app.logger.setLevel(logging.INFO)
formatter = logging.Formatter('%(asctime)s - %(name)s - %(levelname)s - %(message)s')
file_handler = logging.FileHandler('app.log')
file_handler.setFormatter(formatter)
app.logger.addHandler(file_handler)

@app.route('/')
def index():
    app.logger.info('Index route accessed')
    return 'Hello, World!'

if __name__ == '__main__':
```

```
app.run(debug=True)
```

Analyzing Logs for Troubleshooting

Once your Flask API is deployed and logging messages, you can analyze logs to troubleshoot issues and identify areas for optimization. Here are some common log analysis techniques:

1. Search and Filtering: Use tools like grep, awk, or built-in log analysis features in logging platforms to search for specific log messages and filter logs based on criteria such as severity level, timestamp, or source.

2. Aggregation and Visualization: Aggregate log data from multiple sources and visualize logs using tools like Elasticsearch, Logstash, and Kibana (ELK stack) or centralized logging platforms like Splunk or Sumo Logic. This allows you to gain insights into trends, patterns, and anomalies in your log data.

3. Correlation and Tracing: Correlate log messages across different components of your Flask API (e.g., web server logs, database logs) to trace the flow of requests and identify bottlenecks or errors in your application.

4. Alerting and Monitoring: Set up alerts and notifications based on specific log events or conditions using monitoring and alerting tools. This allows you to respond to critical issues or anomalies in real-time and minimize downtime or service disruptions.

Best Practices for Monitoring and Logging

Here are some best practices for effective monitoring and logging in Flask APIs:

1. Define Metrics and KPIs: Define key performance indicators (KPIs) and metrics to monitor the health and performance of your Flask API, such as request latency, error rate, and throughput.

2. Monitor Infrastructure: Monitor infrastructure components (e.g., servers, databases, networking) in addition to your Flask API to identify issues that may impact performance or availability.

3. Log Aggregation: Aggregate logs from multiple sources into a centralized logging platform to simplify log analysis and troubleshooting, especially in distributed or microservices-based architectures.

4. Automate Alerting and Notifications: Set up automated alerts and notifications based on predefined thresholds or conditions to proactively identify and respond to issues in your Flask API.

5. Regular Review and Analysis: Regularly review and analyze logs to identify patterns, trends, and areas for optimization in your Flask API. This helps improve performance, reliability, and user experience over time.

Monitoring and logging are critical components of maintaining a healthy and reliable Flask API in production environments. By setting up effective monitoring tools like Prometheus and Grafana, configuring logging in your Flask API, and analyzing logs for troubleshooting, you can ensure that your API performs optimally and meets the needs of your users. By following best practices for monitoring and logging, you can proactively detect and address issues, optimize performance, and deliver a seamless user experience. Remember to continuously monitor and analyze your Flask API to identify areas for improvement and maintain the highest standards of reliability and performance.

Chapter 9

Clean Coding Principles: Writing Code You (and Others) Can Love

Readability and Maintainability: Keeping Your Code Clean and Clear

Clean coding principles are essential for writing maintainable, readable, and efficient Flask APIs. In this guide, we'll explore best practices for clean coding in Python API development with Flask, focusing on readability and maintainability. We'll cover techniques for writing clear, organized, and understandable code, along with code examples to illustrate each principle.

Readability and Maintainability

Readability and maintainability are key aspects of clean coding. Writing code that is easy to understand and modify not only improves productivity but also reduces the likelihood of introducing bugs and errors. Here are some best practices for improving readability and maintainability in Flask API development:

1. Follow PEP 8 Guidelines

PEP 8 is the official style guide for Python code. Following PEP 8 guidelines ensures consistency and readability across your Flask API codebase. Some key points from PEP 8 include:

- Use consistent indentation (typically 4 spaces).

- Limit lines to 79 characters to improve readability.

- Use descriptive variable and function names.

- Follow naming conventions for classes, functions, and variables.

Example:

```python
# Good
def calculate_area(length, width):
    return length * width

# Bad
def calc_area(l, w):
    return l * w
```

2. Use Meaningful Comments

Use comments sparingly to explain complex logic, algorithms, or non-obvious code. Comments should provide context and explain the why behind the code, not just repeat what the code does.

Example:

```python
# Calculate the area of a rectangle
def calculate_area(length, width):
    # Multiply length by width to get the area
    return length * width
```

3. Modularize Your Code

Break down your Flask API code into smaller, reusable components such as functions or classes. Modular code is easier to understand, test, and maintain than monolithic code.

Example:

```python
# Separate routes into different modules
from app.routes import user_routes, auth_routes
from app.models import User
```

```
app.register_blueprint(user_routes.bp)
app.register_blueprint(auth_routes.bp)
```

4. Use Meaningful Variable and Function Names

Choose descriptive names for variables, functions, and classes that accurately reflect their purpose and functionality. Avoid using single-letter variable names or cryptic abbreviations.

Example:

```python
# Good
def calculate_area(length, width):
    return length * width

# Bad
def calc_area(l, w):
    return l * w
```

5. Keep Functions and Methods Small

Follow the single responsibility principle (SRP) and keep functions and methods small and focused on a single task. Small functions are easier to understand, test, and debug than large, complex ones.

Example:

```python
# Good
def calculate_area(length, width):
    return length * width

def calculate_perimeter(length, width):
    return 2 * (length + width)

# Bad
def calculate_area_and_perimeter(length, width):
    area = length * width
    perimeter = 2 * (length + width)
    return area, perimeter
```

6. Use Docstrings for Documentation

Use docstrings to document modules, classes, functions, and methods in your Flask API code. Docstrings provide documentation and usage examples, making it easier for other developers (including your future self) to understand and use your code.

Example:

```python
def calculate_area(length, width):
    """
    Calculate the area of a rectangle.

    Args:
        length (float): The length of the rectangle.
        width (float): The width of the rectangle.

    Returns:
        float: The area of the rectangle.
    """
    return length * width
```

By following these clean coding principles, you can write maintainable, readable, and efficient Flask APIs that are easy to understand, modify, and maintain. Prioritize readability and maintainability in your codebase to improve collaboration, reduce bugs, and increase productivity. Remember that clean coding is not just about writing code that works—it's about writing code that you (and others) can love.

Code Formatting and Linting: Enforcing Consistency and Style

Code formatting and linting play a crucial role in maintaining consistency, readability, and quality in Flask API development. In this guide, we'll explore the importance of code formatting and linting, best practices for enforcing consistency and style, and how to integrate code formatting and linting tools into your Python Flask API development workflow.

Importance of Code Formatting and Linting

Code formatting and linting are essential for several reasons:

1. Consistency: Ensures consistent coding style and formatting across your Flask API codebase, making it easier to read and understand for both you and other developers.

2. Readability: Improves readability by enforcing clear and concise coding conventions, such as naming conventions, indentation, and spacing.

3. Quality: Identifies potential errors, bugs, and code smells early in the development process, leading to higher-quality code and fewer issues in production.

4. Maintainability: Facilitates code maintenance and collaboration by providing guidelines and standards for writing, reviewing, and modifying code.

Code Formatting with Black

Black is a popular code formatting tool for Python that automatically formats your code to adhere to PEP 8 guidelines. It ensures consistent and uniform code style without requiring manual intervention. Let's see how to use Black in Flask API development:

Installation:

```bash
pip install black
```

Usage:

Run Black on your Flask API codebase:

```bash
black .
```

Linting with Flake8

Flake8 is a linting tool for Python that checks your code for style, syntax, and logical errors. It combines several linting tools, including Pylint, PyFlakes, and McCabe, to provide comprehensive code analysis. Let's integrate Flake8 into our Flask API development workflow:

Installation:

```bash
pip install flake8
```

Usage:

Run Flake8 on your Flask API codebase:

```bash
flake8 .
```

Integrating Code Formatting and Linting into Your Workflow

To ensure consistent code formatting and style in your Flask API development workflow, consider integrating code formatting and linting tools into your version control system, continuous integration (CI) pipeline, and code editor. Here's how you can do it:

1. Version Control Hooks: Set up pre-commit hooks in your version control system (e.g., Git) to run code formatting and linting checks automatically before committing changes. This prevents poorly formatted or problematic code from being committed to the repository.

2. CI Pipeline: Configure your CI pipeline (e.g., GitHub Actions, Travis CI) to run code formatting and linting checks as part of the automated build and test process. This ensures that all code changes are automatically checked for compliance with coding standards before deployment.

3. Editor Integration: Install plugins or extensions for your code editor (e.g., VS Code, PyCharm) that support code formatting and linting. These plugins provide real-time feedback and suggestions, making it easier to adhere to coding standards while writing code.

Best Practices for Code Formatting and Linting

Here are some best practices for using code formatting and linting tools effectively in Flask API development:

1. Use Default Configurations: Start with the default configurations for code formatting and linting tools and customize them as needed to fit your project's requirements.

2. Run Checks Automatically: Set up automated checks to run code formatting and linting checks automatically as part of your development workflow, rather than relying on manual intervention.

3. Address Issues Promptly: Address code formatting and linting issues promptly as they arise to prevent them from accumulating and becoming harder to fix later.

4. Collaborate and Communicate: Collaborate with your team members to establish coding standards and guidelines, and communicate the importance of code formatting and linting for maintaining code quality and consistency.

5. Continuously Improve: Continuously evaluate and update your code formatting and linting configurations to reflect changes in coding standards, best practices, and project requirements.

Code formatting and linting are essential practices in Flask API development for maintaining consistency, readability, and quality in your codebase. By integrating code formatting and linting tools like Black and Flake8 into your development workflow, you can ensure that your Flask API adheres to coding standards, identifies potential issues early, and produces high-quality, maintainable code. Prioritize code formatting and linting as part of your development process to improve collaboration, productivity, and code quality in your Flask API projects.

Documentation: The User Manual for Your API

Documentation is the user manual for your API, providing valuable information on how to use, understand, and interact with your Flask API effectively. In this guide, we'll discuss the importance of documentation, best practices for writing documentation for Flask APIs, and how to generate and maintain documentation using tools like Swagger and Sphinx.

Importance of Documentation

Documentation is crucial for several reasons:

1. User Guidance: Helps users understand how to use your API, including endpoints, request parameters, response formats, and error handling.

2. Onboarding: Facilitates the onboarding process for new developers, providing them with the information they need to start using your API quickly and efficiently.

3. Reference: Serves as a reference guide for developers, providing detailed explanations and examples for each API endpoint and functionality.

4. Troubleshooting: Assists users in troubleshooting issues and errors, guiding them through common problems and solutions.

5. Promotion and Adoption: Acts as a promotional tool for your API, showcasing its features, capabilities, and benefits to potential users and stakeholders.

Writing Documentation for Flask APIs

When writing documentation for Flask APIs, consider the following best practices:

1. Use Clear and Consistent Language: Write in clear, concise language that is easy to understand for users with varying levels of technical expertise. Use consistent terminology and formatting throughout the documentation.

2. Provide Examples: Include code examples and usage scenarios to demonstrate how to use each API endpoint and functionality effectively. Examples help users understand the expected input, output, and behavior of the API.

3. Document Endpoints and Parameters: Document each API endpoint, including its URL, HTTP method, request parameters, request body (if applicable), and response format. Provide detailed explanations for each parameter, including data types, allowed values, and default values.

4. Include Error Handling Information: Document common error responses and status codes returned by the API, along with explanations of each error condition and possible resolutions.

5. Organize Information Effectively: Organize the documentation logically, using sections, headings, and navigation links to guide users through different topics and sections. Make it easy for users to find the information they need quickly.

Generating Documentation with Swagger

Swagger is an open-source framework for designing, documenting, and testing APIs. It provides tools for generating interactive API documentation, allowing users to explore and interact with your API directly from their browser. Let's see how to generate documentation for a Flask API using Swagger:

Installation:

```bash
pip install Flask-Swagger
```

Usage:

```python
from flask import Flask
from flask_swagger import swagger

app = Flask(__name__)

@app.route("/spec")
def spec():
    swag = swagger(app)
    swag['info']['title'] = "My Flask API"
    swag['info']['version'] = "1.0"
    return swag

if __name__ == "__main__":
    app.run(debug=True)
```

```

Access the Swagger UI by visiting `/swagger-ui` in your browser.

**Generating Documentation with Sphinx**

Sphinx is a documentation generation tool widely used in the Python community. It supports multiple output formats, including HTML, PDF, and ePub, making it suitable for generating comprehensive documentation for Flask APIs. Let's see how to generate documentation using Sphinx:

**Installation**:

```bash
pip install sphinx
```

Usage:

1. Initialize a new Sphinx project:

```bash
sphinx-quickstart
```
```

2. Write documentation using reStructuredText (reST) markup in `.rst` files.

3. Build the documentation:

```bash
make html
```

4. View the generated documentation in the `_build/html` directory.

Best Practices for Maintaining Documentation

Here are some best practices for maintaining documentation for Flask APIs:

1. Keep Documentation Up-to-Date: Update the documentation regularly to reflect changes in the API, including new endpoints, parameters, and functionalities.

2. Review and Revise: Review the documentation periodically to ensure accuracy, clarity, and completeness. Revise and improve the documentation based on feedback from users and stakeholders.

3. Versioning: Maintain separate documentation for different API versions, clearly indicating which version of the API each documentation page corresponds to.

4. Provide Changelog: Include a changelog or release notes in the documentation to inform users about changes, enhancements, and bug fixes in each API release.

5. Solicit Feedback: Encourage users to provide feedback on the documentation, including suggestions for improvements, clarifications, and additional information they would find helpful.

Documentation is the user manual for your Flask API, providing valuable information on how to use, understand, and interact with your API effectively. By following best practices for writing, generating, and maintaining documentation, you can ensure that your Flask API documentation is comprehensive, accurate, and user-friendly. Whether you choose to use tools like Swagger or Sphinx, prioritize documentation as an integral part of your Flask API development process to promote adoption, facilitate onboarding, and support user success.

Chapter 10

Flask Extensions: Supercharge Your Development with Powerful Tools

Flask-RESTful: Streamlining RESTful API Development

Flask extensions are third-party libraries that enhance the functionality of Flask and simplify common tasks in web development. In this guide, we'll explore one of the most popular Flask extensions, Flask-RESTful, which streamlines the development of RESTful APIs in Python Flask applications. We'll discuss its features, installation, usage, and best practices for building RESTful APIs with Flask-RESTful.

Introduction to Flask-RESTful

Flask-RESTful is an extension for Flask that adds support for quickly building RESTful APIs using simple, declarative syntax. It provides features for defining resources, routing requests to the appropriate endpoints, parsing request data, and serializing response data, making it easier to build robust and scalable APIs in Flask.

Features of Flask-RESTful

Flask-RESTful offers several features that simplify RESTful API development:

1. Resourceful Routing: Define resources as Python classes and map them to URL endpoints using Flask's routing system. Flask-RESTful automatically handles routing requests to the appropriate resource methods based on HTTP methods (e.g., GET, POST, PUT, DELETE).

2. Request Parsing: Parse request data (e.g., JSON payloads, query parameters, form data) into Python objects using Flask-RESTful request parsing capabilities. This simplifies the process of extracting data from incoming requests and validating input data.

3. Response Serialization: Serialize Python objects (e.g., dictionaries, lists) into JSON responses using Flask-RESTful response serialization features. This makes it easy to format and return data in a consistent and standardized format.

4. Error Handling: Handle errors and exceptions gracefully using the Flask-RESTful error handling mechanism. Customize error messages and status codes for different error conditions to provide informative responses to clients.

Installation

You can install Flask-RESTful using pip, the Python package manager:

```bash
pip install flask-restful
```

```

## Usage

Let's see how to use Flask-RESTful to create a simple RESTful API in a Flask application:

**Example: Creating a Flask-RESTful API**

```python
from flask import Flask

from flask_restful import Api, Resource, reqparse

app = Flask(__name__)

api = Api(app)

# Define a resource class

class HelloWorld(Resource):

    def get(self):

        return {'message': 'Hello, World!'}

# Add the resource to the API

api.add_resource(HelloWorld, '/')

if __name__ == '__main__':

    app.run(debug=True)

```

Best Practices for Building RESTful APIs with Flask-RESTful

Here are some best practices for building RESTful APIs with Flask-RESTful:

1. Use Resourceful Routing: Define resources as Python classes and map them to URL endpoints using Flask-RESTful routing system. Organize your API endpoints logically based on resource types and relationships.

2. Leverage Request Parsing: Use Flask-RESTful request parsing capabilities to extract and validate data from incoming requests. Define request parsers for each resource to specify expected request parameters, data types, and validation rules.

3. Serialize Responses: Serialize Python objects into JSON responses using Flask-RESTful response serialization features. Define serialization schemas for each resource to control the structure and format of response data.

4. Implement Error Handling: Handle errors and exceptions gracefully using the Flask-RESTful error handling mechanism. Customize error messages and status codes for different error conditions to provide informative responses to clients.
```

5. Implement Authentication and Authorization: Secure your RESTful API by implementing authentication and authorization mechanisms using Flask-RESTful built-in features or integrating with authentication libraries like Flask-JWT.

6. Use Middleware: Extend the functionality of Flask-RESTful by using middleware and hooks to add custom behavior to your API endpoints. Implement middleware for tasks like request logging, request/response validation, and authentication.

Flask-RESTful is a powerful extension for Flask that simplifies the development of RESTful APIs in Python Flask applications. By providing features for defining resources, routing requests, parsing request data, and serializing response data, Flask-RESTful streamlines the process of building robust and scalable APIs. By following best practices for building RESTful APIs with Flask-RESTful, you can create well-designed, maintainable APIs that meet the needs of your application and its users. Whether you're building a simple CRUD API or a complex web service, Flask-RESTful provides the tools you need to supercharge your API development with Flask.

Marshmallow: Effortless Data Serialization and Validation

Marshmallow is a powerful Python library that provides effortless data serialization and validation for Flask APIs. In this guide, we'll explore the features of

Marshmallow, how to integrate it into Flask applications, and best practices for serializing and validating data in API development.

Introduction to Marshmallow

Marshmallow is a lightweight library for object serialization and deserialization in Python. It allows you to define schemas for your data models, specifying how data should be serialized to and deserialized from different formats, such as JSON, YAML, or XML. Marshmallow also provides powerful validation features, allowing you to define validation rules for your data and ensure that it meets certain criteria before being processed further.

Features of Marshmallow

Marshmallow offers several features that simplify data serialization and validation in Flask APIs:

1. Schema Definition: Define schemas for your data models using Marshmallow's schema classes. Schemas specify the structure and format of your data, including field types, validation rules, and serialization/deserialization logic.

2. Data Serialization: Serialize Python objects (e.g., dictionaries, lists) into JSON or other formats using Marshmallow's serialization features. Schemas control the serialization process, converting object attributes into serialized data according to the schema definition.

3. Data Deserialization: Deserialize serialized data (e.g., JSON payloads) into Python objects using Marshmallow's deserialization features. Schemas specify how serialized data should be converted back into Python objects, including data type conversion and validation.

4. Data Validation: Validate input data against predefined rules and constraints using Marshmallow's validation features. Schemas allow you to define validation rules for each field in your data model, ensuring that input data meets certain criteria before being processed further.

5. Nested Schemas: Support for nested schemas allows you to define complex data structures and relationships between objects. Nested schemas enable serialization and validation of nested data structures, such as nested dictionaries or lists of objects.

Installation

You can install Marshmallow using pip, the Python package manager:

```bash

pip install marshmallow

```

Usage

Let's see how to use Marshmallow to define schemas, serialize and deserialize data, and perform validation in a Flask application:

Example: Using Marshmallow in Flask

```python
from flask import Flask, request, jsonify
from marshmallow import Schema, fields, ValidationError

app = Flask(__name__)

# Define a schema for a user object
class UserSchema(Schema):
    username = fields.Str(required=True)
    email = fields.Email(required=True)

# Create an instance of the user schema
user_schema = UserSchema()

# Define an endpoint for creating a new user
@app.route('/users', methods=['POST'])
def create_user():
    # Parse request data and validate against schema
```

```
try:

    data = request.json

    user = user_schema.load(data)

except ValidationError as err:

    return jsonify({'error': err.messages}), 400

# Process the user data (e.g., save to database)

    return jsonify({'message': 'User created successfully'}), 201

if __name__ == '__main__':

    app.run(debug=True)
```

Best Practices for Using Marshmallow in Flask APIs

Here are some best practices for using Marshmallow in Flask API development:

1. Define Separate Schemas: Define separate schemas for input data (e.g., request payloads) and output data (e.g., response payloads) to decouple serialization and validation logic.

2. Use Explicit Field Types: Use explicit field types (e.g., `fields.Str`, `fields.Int`, `fields.Boolean`) to specify the data type of each field in your schema. This ensures that data is serialized and deserialized correctly and helps prevent type-related errors.

3. Perform Input Validation: Perform input validation using Marshmallow's validation features to ensure that input data meets certain criteria before being processed further. Define validation rules for each field in your schema to enforce data integrity and security.

4. Handle Validation Errors Gracefully: Handle validation errors gracefully by catching `ValidationError` exceptions and returning informative error messages to clients. Use HTTP status codes to indicate the nature of the error (e.g., 400 for client errors, 422 for validation errors).

5. Use Nested Schemas for Complex Data: Use nested schemas to serialize and validate complex data structures and relationships between objects. Define nested schemas for nested data structures, such as dictionaries of objects or lists of objects, to maintain data integrity and consistency.

Marshmallow is a powerful library for data serialization and validation in Flask APIs, providing features for defining schemas, serializing and deserializing data, and performing validation. By integrating Marshmallow into your Flask application, you can simplify the process of handling input and output data, ensure data integrity and security, and improve the overall reliability and maintainability of your API. Whether you're building a simple CRUD API or a complex web service,

Marshmallow provides the tools you need to effortlessly serialize and validate data in your Flask API.

Other Useful Extensions for Common Tasks

In addition to Flask-RESTful and Marshmallow, there are several other useful Flask extensions available for common tasks in API development. These extensions provide functionality for authentication, database integration, caching, testing, and more, helping you streamline development and build robust APIs. In this guide, we'll explore some of these extensions, their features, and how to use them in Python API development with Flask.

Flask-JWT-Extended: JSON Web Token Authentication

Flask-JWT-Extended is an extension for Flask that provides JSON Web Token (JWT) authentication support. It allows you to protect routes and endpoints in your Flask API by requiring clients to provide a valid JWT token in their requests. Flask-JWT-Extended also provides features for token generation, token refreshing, and token revocation.

Features:

- JWT token-based authentication
- Token generation, refreshing, and revocation
- Customizable token expiration and validation settings

Installation:

```bash
pip install flask-jwt-extended
```

Usage:

```python
from flask import Flask
from flask_jwt_extended import JWTManager
app = Flask(__name__)
app.config['JWT_SECRET_KEY'] = 'your_secret_key'
jwt = JWTManager(app)
# Protect a route with JWT authentication
@app.route('/protected')
@jwt_required
def protected():
    return jsonify(logged_in_as=current_user), 200
if __name__ == '__main__':
```

```
app.run(debug=True)
```

Flask-SQLAlchemy: Database Integration

Flask-SQLAlchemy is an extension for Flask that provides integration with SQLAlchemy, a powerful SQL toolkit and Object-Relational Mapping (ORM) library for Python. Flask-SQLAlchemy simplifies database operations in Flask applications, allowing you to define database models, execute queries, and manage database connections easily.

Features:

- Integration with SQLAlchemy ORM
- Database model definition using Python classes
- Support for multiple database engines (e.g., SQLite, PostgreSQL, MySQL)

Installation:

```bash
pip install flask-sqlalchemy
```

Usage:

```python
from flask import Flask
```

```
from flask_sqlalchemy import SQLAlchemy

app = Flask(__name__)

app.config['SQLALCHEMY_DATABASE_URI'] = 'sqlite:///example.db'

db = SQLAlchemy(app)

# Define a database model
class User(db.Model):
    id = db.Column(db.Integer, primary_key=True)
    username = db.Column(db.String(80), unique=True, nullable=False)
    email = db.Column(db.String(120), unique=True, nullable=False)

if __name__ == '__main__':
    app.run(debug=True)
```
```

## Flask-Caching: Caching Support

Flask-Caching is an extension for Flask that provides caching support for Flask applications. It allows you to cache the results of expensive operations (e.g., database queries, API requests) to improve performance and reduce response times. Flask-Caching supports multiple
```

caching backends, including in-memory caching, file-based caching, and Redis caching.

Features:

- Support for various caching backends (e.g., in-memory, file-based, Redis)
- Decorator-based caching for views and endpoints
- Fine-grained control over caching options and expiration times

Installation:

```bash
pip install flask-caching
```

Usage:

```python
from flask import Flask

from flask_caching import Cache

app = Flask(__name__)

app.config['CACHE_TYPE'] = 'simple'

cache = Cache(app)

# Cache the result of a view function
```

```
@app.route('/')
@cache.cached(timeout=60)
def index():
    return 'Hello, World!'
if __name__ == '__main__':
    app.run(debug=True)
```

Flask-Testing: Testing Support

Flask-Testing is an extension for Flask that provides testing support for Flask applications. It simplifies the process of writing and executing tests for Flask applications, allowing you to test views, endpoints, and other components of your Flask API easily. Flask-Testing provides features for client testing, request mocking, and assertion helpers.

Features:

- Client testing for Flask applications
- Request mocking and patching for testing endpoints
- Assertion helpers for validating responses and behavior

Installation:

```bash
pip install flask-testing
```

Usage:

```python
from flask import Flask
from flask_testing import TestCase
app = Flask(__name__)
class MyTest(TestCase):
    def create_app(self):
        app.config['TESTING'] = True
        return app
    def test_index(self):
        response = self.client.get('/')
        self.assertEqual(response.status_code, 200)
if __name__ == '__main__':
    app.run(debug=True)
```

```

These are just a few examples of the many useful Flask extensions available for common tasks in API development. By leveraging Flask extensions like Flask-JWT-Extended, Flask-SQLAlchemy, Flask-Caching, and Flask-Testing, you can streamline development, improve performance, and ensure the reliability and scalability of your Flask APIs. Whether you need authentication, database integration, caching, testing, or other functionalities, there's likely a Flask extension available to help you meet your needs. Explore the Flask ecosystem and discover extensions that can supercharge your Flask API development process.
```

Conclusion

In conclusion, Python API development with Flask offers a powerful and versatile framework for building robust and scalable web APIs. With its simplicity, flexibility, and extensive ecosystem of extensions, Flask empowers developers to create captivating and innovative APIs that meet the needs of modern web applications.

Throughout this journey, we've explored various aspects of Flask API development, from session management and role-based access control to testing, documentation, and beyond. We've delved into the world of Flask extensions, discovering tools like Flask-RESTful, Marshmallow, Flask-JWT-Extended, Flask-SQLAlchemy, Flask-Caching, and Flask-Testing, which supercharge development and streamline common tasks.

We've learned how to architect clean and maintainable APIs, following best practices for code organization, readability, and documentation. By prioritizing security, performance, and reliability, we've built APIs that inspire confidence and trust among users and stakeholders.

But our journey doesn't end here. The world of API development is constantly evolving, with new technologies, methodologies, and best practices emerging every day. As we continue to explore and innovate, let's remember the lessons learned and the principles embraced along the way.

Let's remain vigilant in our pursuit of excellence, continually seeking ways to improve our APIs, enhance user experiences, and drive innovation in the digital landscape. Let's harness the power of Flask and Python to create APIs that not only meet the needs of today but also anticipate the challenges of tomorrow.

As we embark on the next phase of our journey, let's do so with passion, creativity, and a relentless commitment to excellence. Together, we can build APIs that captivate, inspire, and shape the future of web development. The possibilities are endless, and the adventure awaits. So let's raise our glasses to Flask, Python, and the endless possibilities of API development. Cheers to the journey ahead!

Appendix

Glossary of terms

Here's a glossary of terms commonly used in Python API development with Flask:

1. Flask: Flask is a lightweight and flexible web framework for Python, designed to make web development simple and scalable. It provides tools and utilities for building web applications and APIs.

2. API: API stands for Application Programming Interface. In the context of Flask, an API refers to a set of endpoints that allow clients to interact with a web application or service programmatically.

3. Endpoint: An endpoint is a specific URL in a web API that represents a resource or functionality. Clients can send requests to endpoints to perform actions or retrieve data from the API.

4. Routing: Routing is the process of mapping URLs to view functions in a Flask application. It determines which view function should handle incoming requests based on the requested URL.

5. View Function: A view function is a Python function in a Flask application that handles incoming HTTP requests and generates responses. Each view function is responsible for processing a specific endpoint and returning an appropriate response.

6. Decorator: A decorator is a Python function that modifies the behavior of another function or method. In Flask, decorators are often used to associate view functions with specific URL endpoints or to add additional functionality to view functions.

7. Request: A request is an HTTP request sent by a client to a server to retrieve or modify data. In Flask, the `request` object represents the incoming HTTP request and provides access to request data such as headers, parameters, and body content.

8. Response: A response is an HTTP response sent by a server to a client in response to an HTTP request. In Flask, the `Response` class represents an HTTP response object and allows developers to set response headers, status codes, and content.

9. Serialization: Serialization is the process of converting Python objects into a format that can be transmitted over a network or stored in a file. In Flask API development, serialization is often used to convert database objects or other data structures into JSON or XML format for transmission over HTTP.

10. Deserialization: Deserialization is the process of converting serialized data back into Python objects. In Flask API development, deserialization is often used to parse and validate incoming request data before processing it further.

11. Middleware: Middleware is software that sits between the client and server in a web application and intercepts and processes incoming requests and outgoing responses. In Flask, middleware can be used to add custom functionality to the request-response cycle, such as authentication, logging, or error handling.

12. Authentication: Authentication is the process of verifying the identity of a user or client making a request to a web API. In Flask API development, authentication mechanisms such as JSON Web Tokens (JWT) or OAuth2 are often used to secure endpoints and restrict access to authorized users.

13. Authorization: Authorization is the process of determining whether a user or client has permission to access a specific resource or perform a specific action within a web API. In Flask API development, authorization mechanisms are often used in conjunction with authentication to enforce access control policies.

14. ORM: ORM stands for Object-Relational Mapping. It is a programming technique that allows developers to map database tables to Python objects and vice versa. In Flask API development, ORMs such as SQLAlchemy are often used to interact with databases and perform CRUD (Create, Read, Update, Delete) operations on database objects.

15. CRUD: CRUD stands for Create, Read, Update, Delete. It refers to the four basic operations that can be performed on database objects: creating new objects, reading existing objects, updating existing objects, and deleting existing objects. In Flask API development,

CRUD operations are commonly used to manipulate data stored in a database.

This glossary provides a foundation for understanding key concepts and terminology in Python API development with Flask. As you continue to explore and build Flask applications and APIs, you'll encounter these terms frequently, and understanding their meanings will help you navigate the world of Flask development more effectively.

Common Flask API Development Pitfalls (and How to Avoid Them!)

Flask is a powerful and flexible framework for building web APIs in Python, but like any other technology, it comes with its own set of pitfalls and challenges. In this guide, we'll explore some common Flask API development pitfalls and discuss strategies for avoiding them.

1. Lack of Proper Error Handling

One common pitfall in Flask API development is insufficient error handling. Failing to handle errors properly can lead to unexpected behavior, security vulnerabilities, and poor user experience. To avoid this pitfall, ensure that your Flask application includes comprehensive error handling logic for various scenarios, such as invalid requests, database errors, and internal server errors.

```python
from flask import Flask, jsonify

app = Flask(__name__)

@app.errorhandler(404)
def not_found(error):
    return jsonify({'error': 'Not found'}), 404
```

```python
@app.errorhandler(500)
def internal_server_error(error):
    return jsonify({'error': 'Internal server error'}), 500

if __name__ == '__main__':
    app.run(debug=True)
```

2. Insecure Authentication and Authorization

Another common pitfall is implementing insecure authentication and authorization mechanisms. Failing to properly secure your API endpoints can leave your application vulnerable to attacks such as SQL injection, cross-site scripting (XSS), and unauthorized access. To avoid this pitfall, use industry-standard authentication and authorization techniques, such as JSON Web Tokens (JWT), OAuth2, and role-based access control (RBAC).

```python
from flask import Flask, jsonify, request

from flask_jwt_extended import JWTManager, jwt_required, create_access_token

app = Flask(__name__)

app.config['JWT_SECRET_KEY'] = 'your_secret_key'
```

```python
jwt = JWTManager(app)

@app.route('/login', methods=['POST'])
def login():
    username = request.json.get('username', None)
    password = request.json.get('password', None)
    if username != 'admin' or password != 'admin':
        return jsonify({'error': 'Invalid username or password'}), 401
    access_token = create_access_token(identity=username)
    return jsonify({'access_token': access_token}), 200

@app.route('/protected', methods=['GET'])
@jwt_required
def protected():
    return jsonify(logged_in_as=current_user), 200

if __name__ == '__main__':
    app.run(debug=True)
```

3. Poor Performance and Scalability

Flask applications can suffer from poor performance and scalability if not designed and optimized properly. Common causes of performance issues include inefficient database queries, excessive resource consumption, and lack of caching. To avoid this pitfall, optimize your Flask application by profiling performance, caching frequently accessed data, and using asynchronous programming techniques where appropriate.

```python
from flask import Flask, jsonify

from flask_caching import Cache

app = Flask(__name__)

cache = Cache(app)

@app.route('/data', methods=['GET'])

@cache.cached(timeout=60)

def get_data():

    # Query data from database

    data = ...

    return jsonify(data), 200
```

```
if __name__ == '__main__':

    app.run(debug=True)
```

4. Overly Complex Architecture

Overly complex architecture is another common pitfall in Flask API development. Building a monolithic or overly layered architecture can lead to code duplication, tight coupling, and difficulty in maintaining and extending the application. To avoid this pitfall, follow the principles of simplicity, modularity, and separation of concerns. Break your application into smaller, more manageable components, and use design patterns like MVC (Model-View-Controller) to organize your code effectively.

5. Lack of Testing Coverage

Insufficient testing coverage is a common pitfall that can lead to bugs, regressions, and unreliable APIs. Failing to test your Flask application thoroughly can result in unexpected behavior and poor user experience. To avoid this pitfall, write comprehensive unit tests, integration tests, and end-to-end tests for your Flask API. Use testing frameworks like unittest, pytest, and Flask-Testing to automate the testing process and ensure that your API behaves as expected under different conditions.

```python
```

```python
import unittest

from flask_testing import TestCase

from app import app

class TestAPI(TestCase):

    def create_app(self):

        app.config['TESTING'] = True

        return app

    def test_get_data(self):

        response = self.client.get('/data')

        self.assertEqual(response.status_code, 200)

        self.assertGreater(len(response.json), 0)

if __name__ == '__main__':

    unittest.main()
```
```

Flask API development offers many benefits, but it also comes with its own set of challenges and pitfalls. By being aware of common pitfalls such as lack of proper error handling, insecure authentication and authorization, poor performance and scalability, overly complex architecture, and lack of testing coverage, you can take
```

proactive steps to avoid them and build reliable, secure, and scalable Flask APIs. By following best practices, writing clean and maintainable code, and continuously testing and optimizing your API, you can ensure that it meets the needs of your users and stakeholders now and in the future.

www.ingramcontent.com/pod-product-compliance
Lightning Source LLC
Chambersburg PA
CBHW031610210526
45464CB00004B/1508